Study Guide

Jesus Christ: The Center of the Bible

Distribute at least one week before the first session.

John 20:31; Genesis 3:1–15; Isaiah 52:13–53:12; Psalm 23; Hebrews 13:8

Resources for Worship

Use these resources for your daily study and at the week's assembly.

Hymn

How firm a foundation, O saints of the Lord,
Is laid for your faith in His excellent Word!
What more can He say than to you He has said
Who unto the Savior for refuge have fled?

Fear not, I am with you, oh, be not dismayed,
For I am your God and will still give you aid;
I'll strengthen you, help you, and cause you to stand,
Upheld by My righteous, omnipotent hand.

When through fiery trials your pathway will lie,
My grace, all-sufficient, will be your supply.
The flames will not hurt you; I only design
Your dross to consume and your gold to refine.

Throughout all their lifetime my people will prove
My sov'reign, eternal, unchangeable love;
And then, when gray hairs will their temples adorn,
Like lambs they will still in my bosom be borne.

John Rippon, alt.

Prayer

Jesus, still lead on
Till our rest be won;
And although the way be cheerless,
We will follow calm and fearless;
Guide us by Your hand
To our Fatherland.
Amen.

Nicolaus L. von Zinzendorf; trans. Jane L. Borthwick, alt.

Digging Deep
My Personal Study for Week 1

Day 1 • Read John 20:31

1. Authors write books for a purpose. A book can entertain, inform, chronicle, comfort, motivate, inspire. The Bible, God's book, does all this … and much more. How does God describe the purpose for His book in John 20:31?

2. What are some benefits you receive as you read the Bible?

3. Most books have a central character or event on which they focus. What do these passages say about the central focus of the Bible?

a. Luke 24:13–27

b. Ephesians 2:19–20

c. Numbers 21:8–9 and John 3:14–15

4. Suppose someone tried to read the Bible not realizing that Jesus is its central focus. What erroneous conclusions might such a person draw from that kind of study?

Day 2 • Read Genesis 3:1–15

5. From Genesis through Revelation, God's work of redemption for His people is the focus. God's plan to save the world from sin and Satan was first revealed in today's reading from Genesis.

a. Carefully reread verses 14–15. How and to whom are these verses a curse?

b. How and to whom is verse 15 a blessed promise?

c. What does this promise, given by God so soon after the first sin, show you about Him and about His message to us in the Bible?

6. Through the ages some Christians have thought of the Old Testament as being primarily about God's Law and His message of judgment. In actuality, the Old Testament is loaded with examples of God's *grace*. We've seen evidence of God's grace already in Genesis 3:15. How is that grace evident in these Old Testament passages?

a. Exodus 14:29–31

b. 2 Samuel 7:11–16; 23:3–5

c. Jeremiah 31:31–34

7. **Challenge question.** From your own reading and study of the Old Testament, what other examples of God's grace come to mind?

Day 3 • Read Isaiah 52:13–53:12

8. Messianic prophecies punctuate the Old Testament with great regularity. When Jesus finally came, He fulfilled these prophecies—each one of them. The New Testament documents the ways in which He did this. While some predictions could have been coincidental, and while our Lord had control over some life events, many fell completely outside the realm of His control. Nonetheless, each prophecy was fulfilled, just as the prophets had declared. The verses from Isaiah (*above*) you will read today are quoted more frequently in the

The Holy Scriptures—God's Word

Distribute at the end of session 1 for use in session 2.

John 1:1–4, 14; 2 Timothy 3:16; Romans 1:16–17; John 8:31–32; Psalm 119:41–48

Resources for Worship

Hymn

Oh, that the Lord would guide my ways
To keep His statutes still!
Oh, that my God would grant me grace
To know and do His will!

Order my footsteps by Your Word
And make my heart sincere;
Let sin have no dominion, Lord,
But keep my conscience clear.

Assist my soul, too apt to stray,
A stricter watch to keep;
If ever I forget Your way,
Restore Your wand'ring sheep.

Make me to walk in Your commands,
A most delightful road;
Nor let my head or heart or hands
Offend against my God.

Isaac Watts, alt.

Prayer

Heavenly Father, Your Word is flawless. We believe the Holy Scriptures are Your Word of love in Jesus to us despite our sin. Your Word has power—power to save and power to change lives. Help us truly love Your Word. Open our hearts so that as we study Your Word it will bring us closer to You. In Jesus' name we pray. Amen.

Digging Deep
My Personal Study for Week 2

Day 1 • Read John 1:1–4, 14

1. *The Bible is God's Word.* This statement is true, but Scripture uses the term *God's Word* also in other ways.

a. What is meant by the "Word" in John 1:1–4, 14?

b. What further information concerning Jesus, the Word, do you gain from 1 John 1:1–2 and 5:11?

c. Read John 14:23–24. What do these verses tell you about the origin of Jesus' words?

2. God has spoken to us in Jesus, the living Word. God also spoke to His people through His Old Testament prophets and through His New Testament evangelists and apostles.

a. Read Zechariah 7. As you do, underline the phrase, repeated again and again, that tells you the source of the prophet's words. What is this phrase?

b. Why do you think the prophet used this phrase so frequently?

c. Read Colossians 1:3–6. What do these verses say about the Word of God as proclaimed by the apostles?

d. In what sense is the sermon spoken by your pastor each week "God's Word" also?

3. God's Word spoken by His Old Testament prophets, by Jesus, and by the apostles and evangelists eventually became God's written Word—the Bible (Holy Scripture). Christian leaders often speak about the importance of being "in the Word." Keeping in mind all that is meant by the "Word of God," what does it mean to you to be "in the Word?"

Day 2 • Read 2 Timothy 3:16

4. At the time the words of 2 Timothy 3:16 were written, the apostle Paul referred primarily to the Old Testament. Today this verse applies to the entire Bible.

a. What does the term *God-breathed* tell you about Scripture's origin?

b. How does 2 Peter 1:20–21 further explain the nature and origin of the Bible?

c. Why is it important *to you* that all of Scripture is God-breathed?

5. **Challenge question.** The direct activity of the Holy Spirit upon the writers of the Bible enabled them to write what God wanted us to know. What joy and excitement can you have knowing that God inspired *people* to write the Bible, rather than having it fall from heaven or delivering it through an angel?

Jesus Christ: The Center of the Bible

Distribute at the end of session 2 for use in session 3.

2 Chronicles 34:1–33; Jeremiah 36:1–32; Nehemiah 8:1–18; Acts 17:10–15; 1 John 4:1–3a

Resources for Worship

Use these resources for your daily study and at the week's assembly.

Hymn

God bless our native land;
Firm may it ever stand
Through storm and night.
When the wild tempests rave,
Ruler of wind and wave,
Do Thou our country save
By Thy great might.

So shall our prayers arise
To God above the skies,
On whom we wait.
Thou who art ever nigh,
Guarding with watchful eye,
To Thee aloud we cry:
God save the state!

Charles T. Brooks, st. 1; John S. Dwight, st. 2; alt.

Prayer

Almighty King of kings, forgive the many sins by which we have disgraced this land. Help us as Christian citizens to bring honor to Your name. May our nation prosper and be a blessing to all the earth. In Jesus' name we pray. Amen.

Digging Deep
My Personal Study for Week 3

Day 1 • Read 2 Chronicles 34:1–33

1. At many times throughout history, including the present, ungodly leadership, idol worship, and other factors have influenced God's people to separate themselves from Him and His Word. Today's text describes one such time.

a. Reread verses 1–13. How did God work through King Josiah to begin to bring His people back to Himself?

b. Hilkiah the priest made an amazing discovery during the temple renovation (verses 14–15). How did Josiah react to this discovery (verses 19–21)?

c. In love and power God worked in the heart of Josiah to produce repentance. What does this incident reveal concerning the importance God places on the written Scriptures and on His people's knowledge of His Word?

2. When the scroll was found in the temple, Josiah sent Hilkiah and other representatives to speak to the prophetess Huldah. Huldah prophesied to these men concerning God's attitude toward His people. Reread verses 23–28. What evidence of God's wrath and of God's grace do you find?

3. a. It may seem incredible that the written Word could have been lost. Yet how do people "lose" God's Word today?

b. What effects, in your own life and in the lives of others, have you noticed when God's Word is neglected (lost)?

4. Note what Josiah did with the scroll once it was found (verses 29–32). How does God actively work today to preserve His Word for His people?

5. *For personal reflection. Sharing optional.* As you close today's study, think of times when you have neglected God's Word. Ask God for His forgiveness in Jesus. Then ask Him for renewed desire to use and share His Word daily.

Day 2 • Read Jeremiah 36:1–32

6. Today's Bible reading recalls a time when Judah's key national leaders rejected God and His Word.

a. At the time of this account, what two serious problems did God's people face? See verse 3, and also refer to Jeremiah 25:1–11.

b. Reread Jeremiah 36:1–4. Even though His people openly rejected Him, God still sought to lead them to repentance. Read 1 Timothy 2:4. Despite human sinfulness and many people's rejection of the Lord and His Word today, what does He still want?

7. Jeremiah 36:4–18 tells us that Baruch wrote down all that God had said through Jeremiah. The account goes on to explain that Baruch read these words to all the people in the Lord's temple (verses 8–18).

a. How did the temple officials react?

b. The people in the temple then asked Baruch how he came to write the word (verse 17). What does this question, as well as verse 18, tell you about God's Word?

c. Why did the temple officials urge Baruch and Jeremiah to "go and hide" (verse 19)? Consider Jeremiah 26:20–23 as you answer.

Jesus Christ: The Center of the Bible

Distribute at the end of session 3 for use in session 4.

1 Corinthians 2:6–16; Exodus 14:21–31 and Psalm 114; Psalm 108

Resources for Worship

Use these resources for your daily study and at the week's assembly.

Hymn

Praise to the Lord, the Almighty, the King of creation!
O my soul, praise Him, for He is your health and salvation!
Let all who hear
Now to His temple draw near,
Joining in glad adoration!

Praise to the Lord, who o'er all things is wondrously reigning
And, as on wings of an eagle, uplifting, sustaining.
Have you not seen
All that is needful has been
Sent by His gracious ordaining?

Praise to the Lord, who will prosper your work and defend you;
Surely His goodness and mercy shall daily attend you.
Ponder anew
What the Almighty can do
As with His love He befriends you.

Praise to the Lord! Oh, let all that is in me adore Him!
All that has life and breath, come now with praises before Him!
Let the amen
Sound from His people again.
Gladly forever adore Him!

Joachim Neander; trans. Catherine Winkworth, alt.

Prayer

O Lord, our Lord, how excellent is Your name in all the earth! I will praise You for the wonders of Your creation and above all for the wonders of Your salvation in Jesus Christ! You are my comfort, my salvation, my strength, and my song. With joy I draw water from the well of salvation. I will call on Your name, make known among the nations what You have done, and sing of Your glorious deeds. In the great Savior's name. Amen.

Digging Deep
My Personal Study for Week 4

Day 1 • Read 1 Corinthians 2:6–16

1. God has given us the Bible to be used. God intends that we read and understand it. God wants us to derive joy and comfort from His Word. But parts of the Bible can be difficult to understand. Even so, we need not rely on our own wisdom as we interpret Scripture.

a. Reread verses 6–10 in today's Bible reading. How does God reveal to us the wisdom contained in the Bible?

b. Verse 7 refers to "God's secret wisdom." What is meant by the term *secret* as used here? Consider Romans 16:25–26 as you answer.

2. a. In 1 Corinthians 2:11–12, Paul uses a logical comparison to help us understand why the Holy Spirit's revelation is essential for the correct interpretation of Scripture. Restate this comparison in your own words.

b. Why is it impossible to understand God's Word without the Holy Spirit? Use verses 14–16 and John 3:1–5 to explain your answer.

Day 2 • Read the passages as directed below

3. When a Bible passage seems difficult, it must be understood in light of other clearer verses of Scripture. In many cases, one passage helps the reader to better comprehend another part. Or, stated succinctly, Scripture interprets Scripture.

Read the following passages, emphases added.

Exodus 13:21—By day the Lord went ahead of them in a pillar of cloud to guide them on their way and by night in a pillar of fire to give them ***light***, so that they could travel by day or night.

Isaiah 9:2—The people walking in darkness have seen a great ***light***; on those living in the land of the shadow of death a ***light*** has dawned.

John 8:12—When Jesus spoke again to the people, He said, "I am the ***light*** of the world. Whoever follows Me will never walk in darkness, but will have the ***light*** of life."

2 Corinthians 4:6—For God, who said, "Let ***light*** shine out of darkness," made His ***light*** shine in our hearts to give us the ***light*** of the knowledge of the glory of God in the face of Christ.

Ephesians 5:8—For you were once darkness, but now you are ***light*** in the Lord. Live as children of ***light***.

1 John 1:5—This is the message we have heard from Him and declare to you: God is ***light***; in Him there is no darkness at all.

a. What insights concerning the word ***light*** did you gain from these passages?

b. If you had read only one of these passages in isolation (e.g., Isaiah 9:2), what impression might you have concerning the word *light*?

c. How did considering all the passages aid your understanding of their meaning?

4. What does this brief study of "light" passages show you concerning the danger of creating doctrines based on one or two passages?

Day 3 • Read Exodus 14:21–31 and Psalm 114

5. The writers of Scripture used many different writing styles. For instance, some parts of the Bible are written as direct narratives. These are much like the history or biography being written even today. For instance, Exodus 14:21–31 is written in a narrative style. It describes a miraculous event.

Figurative Language—The Richness of Scripture

Distribute at the end of session 4 for use in session 5.

Isaiah 55:9–11; Matthew 26:26–29; Luke 15:11–32; Luke 10:25–37; Matthew 13:1–23

Resources for Worship

Use these resources for your daily study and at the week's assembly.

Hymn

Speak, O Lord, Your servant listens,
Let Your Word to me come near;
Newborn life and spirit give me,
Let each promise still my fear.
Death's dread pow'r, its inward strife,
Wars against Your Word of life;
Fill me, Lord, with love's strong fervor
That I cling to You forever!

Oh, what blessing to be near You
And to listen to Your voice;
Let me ever love and hear You,
Let Your Word be now my choice!
Many hardened sinners, Lord,
Flee in terror at Your Word,
But to me, who know my burden,
Show me now Your Word of pardon!

Lord, Your words are waters living,
When my thirsting spirit pleads;
Lord, Your words are bread life-giving,
On Your words my spirit feeds.
Lord, Your words will be my light
Through death's vale, its dreary night;
Yes, they are my sword prevailing,
And my cup of joy unfailing!

Precious Jesus, I entreat You,
Let Your words in me take root;
Let this gift of heav'n enrich me
So that I bring gen'rous fruit:
Never take them from my heart
Till I see You as You are,
When in heav'nly bliss and glory
I will meet You and adore You!

Anna Sophia of Hesse-Darmstadt; trans. George T. Rygh, alt.

Prayer

Almighty King of kings, forgive our neglect of Your precious Word. In these days of spiritual famine, enable us to grow strong in the saving Gospel and share it with those who are starving and dying without it. In Jesus' name we pray. Amen.

Digging Deep
My Personal Study for Week 5

Day 1 • Read Isaiah 55:9–11

1. Good writers of secular literature use figurative language to give their writing depth and richness. In the Bible, God also uses figurative language. This should come as no surprise considering the awesome wisdom of our God, the depth of the truths He communicates in Holy Scripture, and His desire that His Word would powerfully change people's hearts and lives.

Figurative language includes comparisons and contrasts. Most of the time it's intended to create pictures in our minds. One such type of figurative language is the *simile*. A simile is a comparison introduced by the words *like, as,* or *than.*

a. Reread Isaiah 55:9. The word *as* at the beginning of this verse indicates the comparison is a simile. What comparison is being made here?

b. What insight does this comparison give the reader? Consider also the context, particularly verses 6–7, as you answer.

2. a. Reread verses 10–11. What comparison is made by the simile in these verses?

b. What insight does this comparison give the reader?

3. Six other figures of speech appear regularly in Scripture. Study the definitions below. Then read the passages referenced below. Which figure of speech does each employ? What effect does each produce?

Metaphor: compares one thing to another as if it were that thing (e.g., "the Lord God is a sun and shield").

Personification: a word picture that gives animate characteristics to something inanimate (e.g., "the sun smiles on the land").

Anthropomorphism: attributing to God physical, human characteristics (e.g., "the right hand of the Lord is exalted").

Hyperbole: An exaggeration to make a point (e.g., "He had the strength of 20 men.")

Interrogation: a question for emphasis, not intended to be answered (e.g., "Who is a god like our God?")

a. Deuteronomy 11:12

b. Judges 7:12

c. Psalm 98:8

d. Isaiah 26:4

e. Romans 8:31–32

Day 2 • Read Matthew 26:26–29

4. While understanding and identifying figurative language gives us further insight into the meaning of Scripture, it is important **not** to identify language as figurative when it is not.

a. Reread Matthew 26:26–29 carefully, focusing on the words *body* and *blood.* Is there anything in this passage that indicates *body* and *blood* are meant to be understood figuratively? Explain. (Review types of figurative language from day 1 of this study.)

b. In previous lessons of this course we have established the principle Scripture interprets Scripture. Read 1 Corinthians 10:16. How does this passage clarify our Lord's words?

Biblical Types, Symbols, and Poetry— Bringing the Good News of Salvation in a Magnificent Way

Distribute at the end of session 5 for use in session 6.

Genesis 12:1–5; 18:20–33; 22:1–12; Joshua 1:1–9; Revelation 1:1–3; 22:6–7, 12–16; Proverbs 10:1–32; Isaiah 5:1–7

Resources for Worship

Use these resources for your daily study and at the week's assembly.

Hymn

Come, O almighty King,
Help us Your name to sing;
Help us to praise;
Father all-glorious,
In all victorious,
Come and reign over us,
Ancient of Days.

Come, O incarnate Word,
Gird on Your mighty sword;
Our prayer attend.
Come and Your people bless,
And give Your Word success,
And let Your righteousness
On us descend.

Come, holy Comforter,
Your sacred witness bear
In this glad hour!
Your sev'nfold gifts impart;
Rule now in ev'ry heart;
Never from us depart,
Spirit of pow'r.

To the great One in Three
Eternal praises be
Hence evermore!
Your sov'reign majesty
May we in glory see
And to eternity
Love and adore.

source unknown, alt.

Prayer

Almighty God, in Your holy Word You have revealed Yourself to us as the great Three in One (Father, Son, and Holy Spirit). O God the Father, who has created us, continue to preserve and protect us. O God the Son, who has redeemed us, bless us always with Your grace. O God the Holy Spirit, who has sanctified us, keep us ever in the saving faith that we may offer endless praise to the eternal Trinity. Amen.

Digging Deep
My Personal Study for Week 6

Day 1 • Read Genesis 12:1–5; 18:20–33; 22:1–12

1. As we have seen, Jesus Christ is the focus of the entire Bible. We see this often in the Old Testament as we encounter *types*. Types are people, events, offices, or institutions from Old Testament history that foreshadow people, events, offices, or institutions in the New Testament. Because the focus of the New Testament is Jesus' redemptive work, it is logical that many of the types we see in the Old Testament point ahead in history to Jesus.

a. The person of Abraham and many events in his life foreshadow the person of Christ and events in His life. Reread Genesis 12:1–5. Focus on verses 4–5. What did Abraham do when he heard God's command?

b. Read John 8:28–29. What similarities and differences do you note between what we might call Jesus' active obedience and Abraham's?

2. Abraham's action in Genesis 18:20–33 foreshadows another aspect of Christ's work for His people.

a. Why did Abraham do this?

b. Read Hebrews 7:26–27. What makes Jesus an intercessor in ways that Abraham could never be?

3. Genesis 22:1–12 foreshadows the Father's ultimate act of love for us. Compare these verses to John 3:16. What similarities and differences do you see between Isaac's father and Jesus' father?

4. People tend to think of Old Testament characters like Abraham as heroes.

a. What is dangerous about this?

b. Thinking about your study of Abraham as a type of Christ, what is a more helpful way to examine Abraham's life and that of other prominent Old Testament people?

Day 2 • Read Joshua 1:1–9

5. Joshua is another type of Christ whose life is recorded in the Old Testament. This "son of Nun" became the leader of the Israelites after Moses' death. The Greek form of Joshua is *Jesus.*

Both *Joshua* and *Jesus* mean roughly "the Lord saves."

a. What comfort would this name have been for the task Joshua was to do (Joshua 1:6)?

b. Read Joshua 1:13. The "rest" spoken of here implies the security, peace, and well-being God's people would receive when Joshua had led them into Canaan. "Rest" also refers to the spiritual security, peace, and well-being God's Old Testament people had in His promise of the Savior to come.

Examine Hebrews 4:1–10. How does Joshua's leading the Israelites to "rest" in Canaan foreshadow the "rest" into which Jesus leads us?

6. a. **Challenge question**. What other types or shadows of Jesus can you suggest from the Old Testament?

b. Recognizing Old Testament types helps us better understand all of Scripture. But what dangers could arise from searching the Old Testament Scriptures too deeply for types?

Recognizing False Teaching

Distribute at the end of session 6 for use in session 7.

Colossians 2:8–10; 1 Thessalonians 1:1–10; 2 Corinthians 4:1–7; Genesis 1:26–27; Ephesians 2:1–10

Resources for Worship

Use these resources for your daily study and at the week's assembly.

Hymn

Draw us to You,
And we will do
What You have taught forever
And hasten on
Where You have gone
To be with You, dear Savior.

Draw us to You
Each day anew.
Let us depart with gladness
That we may be
Forever free
From sorrow, grief, and sadness.

Draw us to You
That we stay true
And walk the road to heaven.
Direct our way
Lest we should stray
And from Your paths be driven.

Draw us to You;
Our hope renew;
Into Your kingdom take us.
Let us all there
Your glory share;
Your saints and joint heirs make us.

Friedrich Funcke; trans. August Crull, alt.

Prayer

Lord Jesus, our ascended Lord, we rejoice that You now rule over us and protect us. Continue to supply Your church with faithful pastors and teachers. Help parents to lead their children in the way of life. Awaken the unconverted and those who have fallen away. Comfort all who are in need. When You come again in glory, grant that together with all believers we may inherit the kingdom You have prepared for us. Amen.

Digging Deep
My Personal Study for Week 7

Day 1 • Read Colossians 2:8–10

1. False interpretations of God's Word and challenges to the truth of His Word are nothing new. (Recall Genesis 3:1.) Again and again through history Satan has attacked basic biblical truths in five main areas. Each day this week we will study one of these five areas. Today we will examine the nature of Christ.

a. Verse 8 in today's Bible reading spells out the main purpose for Paul's entire letter to the church at Colosse. Why did Paul write this letter? (See also verse 4.)

b. The Colossian Christians faced a false teaching we now know as early Gnosticism. It held that physical matter was evil, that the human body was thus evil and detracted from true spirituality, and that a series of angels mediated between a holy, distant creator god and his evil creation. How do you suppose this philosophy would have viewed Jesus Christ?

2. Reread verses 9–10.

a. Also read 1:15–23. What evidence of Jesus as true God and true man do you find in these verses?

b. So what? What's the danger here? In other words, why might Satan continue through the centuries to attack the truth about the nature of Christ?

3. Still today, Satan attacks the truth of who Christ is and what He came to do. Give one or two examples from your own experience.

4. No cult regards Christ as God come in the flesh. What does this tell you about cults?

Day 2 • Read 1 Thessalonians 1:1–10

Just as Satan attacks the nature of Christ, so he also lies about the nature of God. The church at Thessalonica was made up of believers who had turned from the worship of idols to "serve the living and true God" (1:9).

5. a. In the section of Paul's letter to the Thessalonians offered for today's Bible reading, where do you see evidence that the true God is triune?

b. What is revealed in these verses about each specific person of the Trinity?

6. The triune God changed the lives of the Thessalonian believers literally forever!

a. What evidence revealed this change?

b. *For personal reflection. Sharing optional.* How has God worked in your life to make you a model for others?

7. Paul's preaching of the Gospel and the Thessalonians' belief in it prompted great jealousy among the Jews in that region (Acts 17:1–10). So intense was their hatred that a murder plot was hatched against Paul and Silas. When Paul and Silas left for Berea, the persecution against Christians in Thessalonica persisted (1 Thessalonians 1:6).

Bible Translations

Distribute at the end of session 7 for use in session 8.

Romans 5:12–21; 1 Peter 1:18–25; 1 Peter 3:18–22; Psalm 146; Psalm 119:9–16

Resources for Worship

Hymn

Amazing grace!
How sweet the sound
That saved a wretch like me!
I once was lost but now am found,
Was blind but now I see!

The Lord has promised good to me,
His word my hope secures;
He will my shield and portion be
As long as life endures.

Through many dangers, toils, and snares
I have already come;
His grace has brought me safe so far,
His grace will see me home.

Yes, when this flesh and heart shall fail
And mortal life shall cease,
Amazing grace shall then prevail
In heaven's joy and peace.

John Newton, alt.

Prayer

Almighty God, send Your Holy Spirit to us so that we might humbly confess our many sins and by faith take hold of Your precious Gospel promises. Bless the preaching of the Law and Gospel throughout the world. With our hearts warmed by the Good News of salvation, move us to love others and to share the Gospel with them. Help us to live each new day for Him who died for us. We ask this in our Savior's name. Amen.

Digging Deep
My Personal Study for Week 8

Note: For this week's study, you will need one major translation of the Bible in addition to the one you usually use. Major translations include the New International Version (NIV), the New Revised Standard Version (NRSV), the King James Version (KJV), the New King James Version (NKJV), and the New American Standard Bible (NASB).

Day 1 • Read Romans 5:12–21

Last week we explored five foundational doctrines of the Christian faith. Would these doctrines change if you were to use a different translation of the Bible? We will explore that question this week.

1. Read today's Bible reading from at least two different major translations. What facts are common to these verses regardless of the Bible translation you use?

2. a. Do you notice any differences between the translations you read? If so, what are they?

   b. Do the differences you noted change in any way the meaning of the doctrine of justification by God's grace through faith in Christ Jesus? Explain.

3. Based on your study in questions 1 and 2, what can you conclude regarding Bible versions and the doctrine of justification?

Day 2 • Read 1 Peter 1:18–25

4. As you did on day 1 of this study, read today's Bible reading from at least two major translations. What facts included in these verses are the same regardless of the translation you used?

5. a. As you compared these verses, you may have noted that different translations have chosen different words for use in verses 18 and 23. The NIV (New International Version) uses the words *perishable* and *imperishable* where the NKJV (New King James Version) uses *corruptible* and *incorruptible.* While these differences do not change the meaning of the verses, how does the use of them enhance your understanding of the change Jesus has worked in you?

b. You may have noted another difference in verse 20. The NIV uses *chosen* where the NKJV uses *foreordained.* How does considering both words help you better understand the meaning of the verse?

c. What benefits do you see in reading and comparing two major translations of the Bible as you undertake an in-depth study?

6. **Challenge question.** Between 1590 and 1608, William Shakespeare wrote the bulk of his famous plays. In 1611, the King James Version of the Bible was introduced. Here are two passages. One from Shakespeare's Macbeth, the other from the King James Version of Isaiah. Read them both.

What hands are here? Ha! They pluck out mine eyes! Will all great Neptune's ocean wash this blood clean from my hand? No. This my hand will rather the multitudinous seas incarnadine, making the green one red.

Macbeth; William Shakespeare

Thus saith thy Lord the Lord, and thy God that pleadeth the cause of his people, Behold, I have taken out of thine hand the cup of trembling, even the dregs of the cup of my fury; thou shalt no more drink it again.

Isaiah 51:22 KJV

a. What problems or difficulties do English-speaking people today encounter as they read works written from the 17th century?

b. What is the benefit in having the Bible accurately translated into more contemporary versions?

Day 3 • Read 1 Peter 3:18–22

7. Once again, read today's text from at least two major translations. What truths about Baptism do you note?

Reading the Scriptures

Distribute at the end of session 8 to use in session 9.

John 4:1–14; 7:37–39; Romans 10:17; Exodus 2:1–25; Psalm 19; Philippians 3:12–21

Resources for Worship

Hymn

Once He came in blessing,
All our sins redressing;
Came in likeness lowly,
Son of God most holy;
Bore the cross to save us;
Hope and freedom gave us.

Still He comes within us;
Still His voice would win us
From the sins that hurt us;
Would to truth convert us
From our foolish error
Ere He comes in terror.

Thus, if we have known Him,
Not ashamed to own Him,
Nor have spurned Him coldly
But will trust Him boldly,
He will then receive us,
Heal us, and forgive us.

Those who then are loyal
Find a welcome royal.
Come, then, O Lord Jesus,
From our sins release us;
Let us here confess You
Till in heav'n we bless You.

Johann Horn; trans. Catherine Winkworth, alt.

Prayer

Jesus Christ, do not delay,
But hasten our salvation;
We often tremble on our way
In fear and tribulation.
Oh, hear and grant our fervent plea;
Come, mighty Judge, and set us free
From death and every evil. Amen.

Digging Deep
My Personal Study for Week 9

Day 1 • Read John 4:1–14; 7:37–39

1. Today's Bible reading points out the greatest benefit we receive from Jesus, the Word. This benefit is the one from which all other blessings of Christ's kingdom flow. What is this benefit?

2. During week 1 of this study, you listed benefits you've received as you've studied God's Word. Look back at your list (week 1, day 1, question 2). Based on today's Bible reading and the past eight weeks of study, what other benefits might you add to your original list?

Day 2 • Read Romans 10:17

3. The Bible speaks in many places of "hearing" the Word. Today's reading is but one of these examples. "Hearing" as used in this text includes much more than the physical action of sound waves bouncing off the eardrum. What does this verse say about "hearing"? (See also a description of the opposite, "not hearing," in Isaiah 30:8–15.)

4. *For personal reflection. Sharing optional.* When is it difficult for you to truly "hear" God's Word? Describe specific circumstances that cause such "deafness" for you.

5. We never read and study the Bible alone; always the Holy Spirit partners with us to open the Scriptures to our hearts.

   a. According to 1 Corinthians 2:13–16, how does the Holy Spirit help us as we read the Scripture?

   b. God "saved us through the washing of rebirth and renewal by the Holy Spirit" (Titus 3:5). How do you see this renewing work going on in you as you read and study the Bible?

Day 3 • Read Exodus 2:1–25

6. Perhaps you're wondering how to develop an effective personal plan of Bible study. Share with others in your small group one or more of the personal Bible study strategies that have worked well for you. Be specific about times, places, habits, reading plans, devotional guides, and other tools that have helped you.

7. When we read the Bible, it often helps to have some basic questions in mind. These general guidelines can help us dig out the main points of a text. Today's Bible reading is an example of an Old Testament historical account. Study the text closely using these questions:

   a. Where is God's care and preservation of His people evident in this text?

   b. What hints, if any, do you see of God's future deliverance in Jesus, the Savior?

   c. Where does God's Law confront you in this passage? In other words, where do you see your need, sins, or failures?

   d. Where in this passage do you see the Gospel—God's forgiveness, provision, and strength for you?

e. Think about the four questions you just answered (a–d). How could these questions help you read and explore other Old Testament historical texts?

8. The two key doctrines of all of Scripture are Law and Gospel. The Law reveals our sin and makes God's wrath at our disobedience clear. The Gospel reveals Jesus the Savior and what God has done and continues to do for us in Jesus. How can identifying Law and Gospel in each text we read unlock the meaning of the Scripture for our individual lives?

Day 4 • Read Psalm 19

9. In week 6 of this course we looked at the use of descriptive language. We also saw that the writers of Scripture's poetic books used parallelism rather than the rhythm of rhyme we usually associate with poetry. Look back at the study leaflet for week 6 and consider the following questions as you study Psalm 19.

a. What descriptions, comparisons, or contrasts stand out for you as you read this psalm?

b. Where do you see Jesus in this psalm?

c. Psalms are prayers. In this psalm, about what, or for what, is the psalmist praying?

d. What situations or events in your life have caused you to have similar thoughts or to pray a prayer similar to this one?

10. The four gospels tell the facts of Jesus' life and ministry. The word *gospel* means "good news." These first four books of the New Testament tell the best news of all: Jesus came to earth to keep God's Law in our place; He died on the cross to save mankind from their sins; and He came alive again to give us eternal life. In the gospels we see the fulfillment of God's Old Testament promises. Read *one* of the following Gospel accounts: Matthew 8:23–27; Mark 4:35–41; or Luke 8:22–25. Delve into the text you chose with the aid of these four questions.

a. Briefly summarize Jesus' actions in this text.

b. What does the text reveal to you about Jesus?

c. What does the text reveal to you about yourself?

d. Where is God's grace evident in this text?

e. How could these four questions guide your reading in the gospels (Matthew, Mark, Luke, John)?

Day 5 • Read Philippians 3:12–21

11. The epistles are letters written by the apostles to individuals and/or churches after Jesus ascended into heaven. These letters proclaim Christ and provide instruction on how to live our lives in Him by the power of the Holy Spirit. They are practical books that encourage and uplift us. Use the following questions to help you understand today's Bible reading from Paul's letter to the Philippians.

a. What are the setting and purpose of this text? (Hint: Consider the context by reading the surrounding verses, especially 4:10–19. Also look at the beginning verses of the book as you answer.)

b. What truths concerning Jesus are proclaimed in this text?

c. What warnings and/or encouragements for your daily life do you find in this reading?

12. Take time now to pray, asking God for His help and encouragement to keep you studying His Word on a regular basis. Following your prayer, outline a basic Bible reading plan you can use during the next 30 days. Consider the following questions as you develop your plan.

- When will I schedule daily time to be with the Lord in His Word?
- Where would I like to begin? Old or New Testament? Genesis to Revelation? Selected parts of the Bible to meet a current need (e.g., comfort, forgiveness, guidance)? Or …?

13. Most books have dust jackets or back cover copy that describes the book's contents. These descriptions are written so that the browser will want to read the entire book. Think over what you've learned about the Bible during the past nine weeks. Consider its theme, purpose, source of inspiration, and the types of writing it contains. Then jot down some statements appropriate for a Bible's back cover. Express your love for God's Word, and try to interest others in reading and studying it.

The questions you've used in days 3 and 4 of this study are printed on pp. 20–21 in the enrichment magazine. You may duplicate them for use in your daily personal Bible study.

8. Rewrite the verses of today's text in your own words.

9. Your answer to question 8 is a *paraphrase*. A paraphrase seeks to explain the meaning of a passage. It often changes, adds, or subtracts words and phrases. A paraphrase is different from a translation in that it does not conform as closely to the original text as does a translation. For a time the most popular version of the Bible in the United States was a paraphrase—*The Living Bible. The Living Bible* renders verse 21 in these words: "That, by the way, is what baptism pictures for us: In baptism we show that we have been saved from death and doom by the resurrection of Christ; not because our bodies are washed clean by the water, but because in being baptized we are turning to God and asking Him to cleanse our *hearts* from sin."

a. What differences do you find between this paraphrase and the Bible translations you are using?

b. Read Ephesians 5:26 and Titus 3:5 from both translations you are using. What does Baptism really do?

c. What caution concerning the use of paraphrased versions of the Bible would you offer based on your experience with 1 Peter 3:20–22?

Day 4 • Read Psalm 146

10. While there are some serious cautions surrounding the use of paraphrased versions of the Bible, paraphrases of Scripture that keep the original intent in mind can be thought-provoking devotional tools. Read the following paraphrase of Psalm 146:

Praise God!
As long as I have breath in my body,
I will praise God!

Don't pin your hopes on the genius of men or women.
Their ultimate end is the same as yours,
and they become once more
like the dust from which they came.
Those who draw their strength from God are secure.
He who created the earth and all upon it
is the only One who can heal the wounds
and mend the fractures of our disjointed world.
He can break the bonds of obsession
and pierce humanity's stupor with visions of truth.
He tenderly reaches out
to those who are oppressed
and reveals His concern
for those who are lost and lonely.
He watches over His own
while the paths of the godless
lead to their own destruction.
This is the God who cannot die!
Praise God!
Amen!

From *Psalms/Now*, prayers and meditations on the Psalms, by Leslie Brandt, CPH, 1974, 1996.

Compare this paraphrase to Psalm 146 in the Bible translation you are using. In what ways does this paraphrase enhance your understanding of the translated version of this psalm?

11. In what kinds of situations would you see such a paraphrased version to be particularly useful?

Day 5 • Read Psalm 119:9–16

12. This week's study has explored the reliability of the major translations of the Bible. Access to Bibles that we can read and understand is a great blessing from God.

a. According to today's Bible reading, what are some of the benefits in studying and living God's Word?

b. How have you experienced these benefits through your own reading and study of the Bible?

c. How would your life be different if you did not have ready access to God's written Word?

13. a. What does the psalmist mean when he says, "I have hidden Your word in my heart" (verse 11)? See also Isaiah 30:20–21 and John 16:12–15.

b. As we read, study, and even memorize the Scripture, the Holy Spirit hides God's Word in our hearts. When your faith is challenged, how does this help you?

14. What confidence do you gain knowing that those who translate the Bible vigorously study the original Greek and Hebrew as they go about their task?

15. Reflecting on this week's study, how would you address an individual who is reluctant to trust any translation of the Bible?

a. Despite their suffering (verse 6), how were the Thessalonian Christians able to continue to welcome the message of the triune God with joy? (Think about the work of each person of the Trinity as you answer.)

b. What comfort does this give you when faced with persecution of any kind because of your Christian faith?

8. So what? What is the danger here? In other words, why might Satan continue through the centuries to attack the doctrine of the Holy Trinity?

Day 3 • Read 2 Corinthians 4:1–7

So far this week we have looked at two basic biblical doctrines: the doctrine of Jesus Christ, true God and true man, and the doctrine of the Trinity. This week's third basic doctrine involves the authority of Scripture. It's familiar since we examined it in week 2. Today we will discuss why and how Satan attacks God's Word.

9. Like the Christians in Colosse and Thessalonica, the Christians in Corinth had to contend with false teachers. In today's Bible reading, Paul contrasts true biblical teaching with the false teaching abundant in Corinth.

a. How did the attitude and motives of Corinth's false teachers differ from the approach of Paul and other true Christian teachers in Corinth?

b. True Christian teaching is based on the authority of God's Word and centers on Christ. How can knowing this help you evaluate any sermon, Bible class, or teaching?

10. Reread verses 6–7. Paul recognized that unless God enlightened his heart, his teaching would be darkness, false. Paul knew the power of his words came from God, not from himself.

As a church gains prominence and increases in size, Satan can try to deceive its human leadership. Satan tries to pollute the group's beliefs and practices with worldly "wisdom" and values. When such practices escalate, followers may ask, "What does the *church* say about ...?" rather than "What does *God* say about ...?" How can the truths in today's Bible reading protect your congregation from this danger?

Day 4 • Read Genesis 1:26–27

11. The two natures of Christ. The doctrine of the Trinity. The authority and power of God's Word. Satan attacks and would destroy each of these doctrines if he could. A fourth teaching he hates is that of the nature of God's human creatures.

How is the Genesis 1 account of the creation of humans different from the New Age view that we partake of the divine nature, that the "spark" of divinity resides in us, and all we need to do to reach our potential is to become aware of it?

12. When God created Adam and Eve they were perfect, as was all of God's creation. Sin, however, changed God's perfect creation. Compare Genesis 1:26–27 to Genesis 5:3–4. How did sin change man's image?

13. Many religious thinkers in today's world believe that our basic flaw is not original sin, but is instead ignorance. If we but understand the "divine stature" that resides in all of us, we would be free, content, healthy, and wise. Or so they claim. These same people conclude that if we look into ourselves and tap into this divine nature, we will find the answers and solutions to the problems in our life.

a. What is wrong about this way of thinking? See Matthew 15:18–20 and Romans 3:23.

b. Read Romans 3:21–26. Where do we find our answers and our hope?

Day 5 • Read Ephesians 2:1–10

14. Today we come to the fifth and most important Christian doctrine, one which Satan attacks most vehemently of all. Verses 8–9 of today's Bible reading express this truth clearly.

a. What is it?

b. Even though Scripture presents this doctrine with great clarity, many people, including some who attend Christian churches, do not know or rely on this truth. How can that happen?

15. Many people strive for self-improvement. They hope that through self-knowledge and determination they will be enlightened and their lives will be transformed. According to Ephesians 2:1–7 and 2 Corinthians 5:14–21 how does true transformation take place?

16. We are saved by God's grace through faith in Christ Jesus. By God's grace we have eternal life now and forever. That same grace helps us in our daily walk in this world. Why would Satan seek to twist this truth above all others?

17. Many today believe that education is the key to society's problems. They hope that as we teach one another to become more understanding and tolerant, the world will become a better place. They may think that God is watching over us—from a distance, but they deny that He takes an active role in our daily lives. They see Jesus as a fine example of how to live a moral life, but they reject any claim that He is true God, true man, the world's Savior. They reject the notion of personal sin and the need for repentance, and focus instead on the need for "enlightenment" or, alternatively, "trying harder" to get along with others. Based on the five truths we studied this week, rewrite this diagnosis of the human condition and its cure.

Day 3 • Read Revelation 1:1–3, 22:6–7, 12–16

Throughout the Bible the holy writers sometimes use symbols. Symbols are much like types in that they can reveal the person and work of Jesus. But whereas types only represent the future, symbols can represent the past and present as well. When correctly interpreted, symbolic language can direct us to remember important promises and truths of God. Symbols can also serve as visual reminders of our faith. For example, the book of Revelation is in large part symbolic. Its use of symbolic language has made it one of the most misinterpreted books of the Bible. In keeping with the principles of interpretation previously discussed (week 4), the symbols used in Revelation should always be interpreted in light of the rest of Scripture.

7. Read the following passages from Revelation and the references in parentheses following each. Note the symbols you find and their meaning.

a. Revelation 7:9, 17 (John 1:29)

b. Revelation 1:16 (Hebrews 4:12)

c. Revelation 1:12, 20 (Matthew 5:14–16)

d. Revelation 21:2 (Jeremiah 3:17)

8. Numbers are also used as symbols throughout Revelation. One frequent example is the number 7. This number is mentioned 52 times in the book.

a. What items numbered in sevens do you note in the following passages?

Revelation 1:4

Revelation 1:12

Revelation 5:1

Revelation 15:1

b. Bible scholars have noted that the number seven indicates totality or completeness. The book of Revelation tells of the completion of God's plan to bring all believers to Himself in our heavenly home. Numbers that add up to seven are sometimes also included in this symbolism. Think about the number associated with the *Triune* God. Now read Revelation 7:1. What else can the number seven (3 plus 4) symbolize?

9. To Bible readers today, the symbols and visions in the book of Revelation may seem strange, confusing, or even frightening. However, God has a very clear reason for giving us this part of the Bible. Review the Bible verses you have studied today. Keeping in mind the truth that all Scripture centers on Christ Jesus, what would you say is the main message or theme of Revelation?

10. At the time Revelation was written (about A.D. 95), Christians faced growing hostility from the surrounding culture. Roman leaders were beginning to demand emperor worship while Christians held that Christ alone is Lord.

a. Knowing this historic fact, why do you think God inspired John to record so much of Revelation using symbolic language?

b. Even though this has been a very brief study of the use of symbolic language in the Scripture, how can you now approach such passages when you encounter them in your Bible reading?

Day 4 • Read Proverbs 10:1–32

11. Job, Psalms, Proverbs, Ecclesiastes, and Song of Solomon are called the poetic books of the Bible. While they were written originally in Hebrew, we read these books in English. Consequently, they may not seem like poetry. They contain little of the rhythm and none of the rhyme we have come to associate with poetry. However, Hebrew poetry consists of a balance of *thoughts* rather than of words and sound patterns. This balance is called parallelism.

There are several types of parallelism. *Synonymous parallelism* expresses the same thought in two or more ways within a single verse. *Antithetic parallelism* presents contrasting or opposing thoughts side by side within a verse. Reexamine Proverbs 10. What type of parallelism do you see used in its verses? Give an example.

12. a. How would you summarize the main idea of this entire chapter?

b. How does the use of poetry help develop this main point in a way that a narrative style would not?

Day 5 • Read Isaiah 5:1–7

13. Other books of the Bible feature poetry prominently. One such book is Isaiah. Chapter 5 begins as a beautiful love poem. It uses figurative language to paint a powerful picture. Keep in mind the features of figurative language you have studied this week. Which do you notice in this poem?

14. Vineyards are used to symbolize Israel throughout Scripture. Jesus' parable of the tenants (Matthew 21:33–44) is believed to be based on Isaiah 5:1–7.

a. Read the parable from Matthew, then compare its symbolism to that of Isaiah. What similarities do you note?

b. How does Jesus' parable further develop the ideas found in Isaiah 5:1–7?

15. A friend who frequently reads his Bible talks to you about his interpretation of certain events and symbols in the Scripture. He says that many biblical events and symbols directly point to specific events happening in China and the Mideast today. Based on this week's study, how would you address such a statement?

c. Can we as humans understand how this can be? Why or why not?

d. What does this tell you about why some people have attempted to explain the Matthew passage as mere figurative language?

5. What dangers can result from misinterpreting factual, narrative language as figurative? See as an example 1 Corinthians 11:27–29.

Day 3 • Read Luke 15:11–32

6. Parables are, in essence, extended figures of speech. The word *parable* comes from the Greek word *parabole* which means "a placing beside" or "a comparison." A parable compares common objects, situations, or people with the truth concerning God and/or His kingdom. In general, each parable makes one main point, one "point of comparison." If we try to interpret each detail, we soon find ourselves out beyond the Scripture's intent.

Every parable has three components: (1) the *setting*—the circumstances that led up to it being told; (2) the *narrative*—the story itself; and (3) the *lesson*—the spiritual truth that lies behind the story.

a. To uncover the setting of the parable featured in today's Bible reading, look back to the first few verses of Luke 15. What do verses 1–2 tell you about why Jesus told this parable?

b. Luke 15:11–32 is actually the third in a series of parables Jesus told concerning the joy of finding that which had been lost. This parable is often called "The Lost Son" or "The Prodigal Son." Neither son in the story, however, is the central focus of the parable. Why might "The Forgiving Father" or "The Father's Love" be more appropriate titles?

c. What lesson—spiritual truth—does this parable communicate?

7. Recall that Jesus told this parable to address criticisms of the Pharisees and others. Realizing this setting, what added dimension does this parable take on?

8. What does this parable say to you?

Day 4 • Read Luke 10:25–37

9. Carefully reread verses 25–28.

a. What is the setting of this parable? See also Matthew 22:34–39, Deuteronomy 6:5, and Leviticus 19:18.

b. To save face after his initial question, the "expert in the law" asks Jesus another question in verse 29. How does this question further define the setting of the parable to follow?

10. Jesus tells a parable to answer the question.

a. Based on the parable, how does Jesus define the term *neighbor*?

b. John 4:9 sheds further light on this parable. How did Jews and Samaritans view one another?

c. Knowing this, how does Jesus' parable become an even more powerful statement of law to the "expert" who is questioning Him?

11. What effect does this parable produce in you?

Day 5 • Read Matthew 13:1–23

12. The "Parable of the Sower" and the verses that follow it (including the parable's explanation) contain much information about why Jesus frequently used this figure of speech in His teaching. What is the setting for this parable?

13. Briefly describe the parable's point (verses 3–9; 18–23).

14. Sandwiched between the parable and its explanation are Jesus' own words explaining why He frequently taught with parables. Reread verses 11–17. Summarize His explanation.

15. There are those who claim the examples of figurative language in the Bible, especially parables, are little more than the simplistic fables of a primitive culture. Based on your study this week, how would you respond to such an idea?

How can you tell that these verses report an actual event, one meant to be taken literally?

6. Psalm 114 describes the same event as Exodus 14, but in a very different way.

a. Reread verses 3–7. Compare them to Exodus 14:21–28. What differences do you note?

b. Obviously the sea cannot look, mountains and hills can't skip, and the earth cannot tremble in fear like a person. Why does the writer use such language?

c. Why is it important to distinguish narrative from poetry as you study Scripture?

7. Among even Christians today, controversy has arisen concerning what is and what is not to be accepted literally in Scripture. Some say, for example, that the world could not have been created in six days. Others say there is no way Shadrach, Meshach, and Abednego could have survived the fiery furnace. Some who consider themselves Christians even insist that Jesus could not have risen bodily from the dead.

a. Why does such controversy arise?

b. Review 1 Corinthians 2:14–16. Also consider 1 Thessalonians 2:13. How does the Holy Spirit help us accept what the Bible says even though at times we may not be able to understand or explain such facts by our own reasoning?

Day 4 • Read the passages as directed below

8. Read 1 Corinthians 15:3–4. Summarize what Paul here says is "of first importance." What makes it so important?

9. Next read Philippians 2:12.

a. Based on only this verse, how would you say we are saved?

b. Now read Philippians 2:1–13 in its entirety. How would you change your previous answer after studying the context of Philippians 2:12?

c. We have seen the principle Scripture interprets Scripture. Another principle is sometimes called the "material principle." It asks the questions, "What is the heart of the matter? What matters most?" The answer, of course, is the doctrine of salvation by grace through faith for Jesus' sake. That is the principle "material" that makes up the Bible. Why must we reject any interpretation of any passage that contradicts this central truth of all Scripture?

10. We often read and hear words out of context today, especially in news reporting. Sound bites drawn from interviews or speeches appear nightly on the news.

a. What can result when a person's statement is taken out of context and shared with the public?

b. Think back to your study today. What have you learned about the importance of context in interpreting the Scripture?

Day 5 • Read Psalm 108

11. Consider the phrase, "Moab is my washbasin, upon Edom I toss my sandal." Whatever can this mean? In cases like this one, knowing the historical setting of a verse or passage can assist the reader in the correct interpretation. Let's work through this phrase as an example.

a. Skim the entire psalm. What is its general theme?

b. Focus now on verse 9. Study a map of Israel and the surrounding nations in the days of David, this psalm's writer. Identify Moab, Edom, and Philistia.

c. Read 2 Samuel 8:1–2, 13. What do these verses tell you about Israel's relationship with Moab, Edom, and Philistia?

d. In David's time, when a nobleman would come home, he would toss his sandals to his servant, much as we might kick off our shoes when we walk in the front door. The servant would then wash the nobleman's feet. Being aware of this custom, what can you deduce concerning the meaning of verse 9?

12. It is also helpful when reading the Bible to have knowledge of the verb tenses used in the original Hebrew and Greek manuscripts. Sometimes our English translations convey this, but sometimes they do not. It's at this point that commentaries can prove helpful.

Read Matthew 10:6. The verb *go* in the original Greek is written in a tense that means to "keep on going." How does knowing this add meaning to the verse?

13. Suppose an acquaintance says to you, "In my opinion, people can make the Bible prove anything." Based on this week's study, how would you respond?

8. As King Jehoiakim heard the word of the Lord, he cut Jeremiah's scroll into pieces and burned it, strip by strip (verse 23). The king showed no fear or remorse. In fact, he ordered the arrest of Baruch and Jeremiah (verses 24–26).

a. How did the Lord preserve His Word despite King Jehoiakim's attempts to destroy it?

b. In what similar situations today do people, particularly those in positions of leadership, reject God's Word or make conscious efforts to destroy it?

9. God worked through Jeremiah to preserve His Word for His people. How does He do that today?

Day 3 • Read Nehemiah 8:1–18

10. During the past two days of study, we've seen God work to preserve His Word for His people despite their neglect, rejection, and overt intent to destroy it. Today's reading opens another facet concerning this preservation.

God's people had spent 70 years in captivity in Babylon. This was 70 years of exile from the public worship of God and the public reading and study of His Word. Following their release, the Jews rebuilt Jerusalem and resettled it and other towns in Israel. On the first day of the seventh month (8:2) the people gathered in Jerusalem for the Feast of Trumpets. This day was also New Year's Day on the civil calendar of this era. Ezra led the people in this festival worship.

As you reread these verses, what strikes you concerning the importance of this occasion and the Word's effect?

11. Verses 11–18 describe the celebration after the worship service. God's Law had brought the people to tearful repentance as they realized their sinfulness and unfaithfulness (verse 9). But hearing of God's covenant promises, especially concerning the Savior to come, brought great joy. We, too, hear Law and Gospel as we read and study the 66 books of the Bible. Why are Law and Gospel each important?

Day 4 • Read Acts 17:10–15

12. We sometimes call the 66 books of the Bible "the canon." The word *canon* means "straight edge" or "ruler."

a. What standard did the Bereans use to measure Paul's teachings, to determine their truthfulness?

b. What attitudes of the Bereans would you most like to emulate? Explain.

13. Consider our culture and the proliferation of cults and "spiritual leaders" today. What do 2 Peter 1:16–18 and 2:1–3 say to us?

Day 5 • Read 1 John 4:1–3a

14. The apostle John reminds us that we need to test all "spirits to see whether they are from God" (verse 1).

a. Why is a healthy skepticism warranted?

b. What specific standard does John urge us to use as we sift truth and falsehood?

15. An acquaintance says, "It is impossible that the Bible tells us all God wants us to know about Him. Many other books should also be considered God's Word." Based on what you've studied this week, especially concerning the ways God has preserved His Word for us, how would you respond to this statement?

Day 3 • Read Romans 1:16–17

6. Throughout history, words people have penned have released slaves, ended conflicts, directed civilization, and fomented revolutions. Human words can uplift, encourage, or destroy. Without a doubt, words are powerful. God's Word contains the very power of the Holy Spirit Himself! No humanly inspired words can ever match that power. What powerful effects of God's Word do these passages describe?

a. Romans 1:16–17

b. Ephesians 6:17

7. The Holy Spirit's power, working in human hearts by means of God's Word, changes people.

a. How have you seen this happen in your own life?

b. How have you seen this happen in the lives of others?

8. **Challenge question.** The sacraments have been called "God's visible Word." Why might this be?

Day 4 • Read John 8:31–32

9. Throughout our lives we search for truth. We want to know the truth about the products we buy, the people with whom we associate, the factors that contribute to good health. But the truth about such subjects can change. Advances in science, further testing, human error, and other factors can make former truths now false, or at least not as true as what was once believed. In today's Bible reading, Jesus talks about *the* truth (verse 32).

a. What is *the* truth? See also John 17:17–19.

b. How does the truth of Scripture differ from human and worldly wisdom? Consider Isaiah 40:8.

10. Almost from the time Adam and Eve took their first breath, God's people have been confronted with temptation to question the truth of God's Word.

a. Skim Genesis 3:1–5. By what techniques did Satan challenge Eve's faith in God's Word? Compare Genesis 2:17 with 3:3.

b. Which of these same schemes does Satan use to challenge your faith in the true Word of God?

11. a. Read Luke 4:1–12. Satan challenged Jesus' belief in the truth as he tried to tempt Him. How did Jesus reply to Satan's temptations? (See verses 4, 8, and 12.)

b. Jesus defeated Satan using the "Sword of the Spirit" (Ephesians 6:17), thus keeping God's law perfectly as our substitute. Because He did, and because He died for us, we can now use that same "sword" to fend off Satan's attacks, his temptations. How can you use the truths of God's Word in your battle with Satan?

Day 5 • Read Psalm 119:41–48

12. a. What words or phrases in today's reading show the psalmist's love and reverence for God's Word?

b. *For personal reflection. Sharing optional.* What place does God's Word hold in your heart?

13. Devotion to God's Word and to the God of the Word is the focus of Psalm 119. One of the most memorable passages of this psalm is verse 105. Read this verse.

a. Without God's Word, where would you be in regard to salvation?

b. How have you found your study of the Bible to be beneficial in your daily living?

14. Suppose an acquaintance said to you, "I don't understand why people call the Bible *God's* Word. The Bible had so many authors over so many years of history, it can't possibly be all that Christians think it is." In light of what you've learned in this week's study, how would you respond to such a comment?

New Testament than any other Old Testament passage. Taken as a unit these 15 verses are often called the "Gospel in the Old Testament." What aspects of Christ's saving work do they describe? As far as is possible, focus on the text from Isaiah and draw your descriptions of Christ's work from the prophet's words and images.

9. Here are a few more Messianic prophecies and the New Testament passages that detail their fulfillment. Jot down what each pair of passages foretells about the Messiah and the way that prophecy was fulfilled in the life of Jesus.

a. Micah 5:2 and Matthew 2:1–6

b. Deuteronomy 18:15, 18–19 and John 7:40

c. Psalm 22:7–8 and Luke 23:11, 35

d. Psalm 69:21 and Matthew 27:34

e. Exodus 12:46 and John 19:31–36

f. Psalm 16:10 and Acts 2:22–32

10. What does the New Testament fulfillment of this many Old Testament prophecies tell you about the written Word of God and the confidence you can have in it? (Think especially about the unity of its message.)

Day 4 • Read Psalm 23

11. In the Bible God paints *pictures* of Jesus—His person and work. These Old Testament pictures vividly portray the coming Messiah. The New Testament picks up many of the same pictures to describe the Lord Jesus. He Himself often uses these pictures. For instance, David records perhaps the most beloved picture of Jesus—in Psalm 23.

a. What does the "shepherd" do for His sheep according to this psalm?

b. In David's time, kings were often called "shepherds." What does this connection add to the picture David used?

c. How is Jesus characterized as a shepherd in the New Testament? See John 10:11, 14; 1 Peter 5:2–4.

12. Another picture of Jesus used throughout the Bible is that of a lamb, the Lamb of God. Read two or more of these passages: Exodus 12:5, 21, John 1:29, and 1 Peter 1:19. What picture of Jesus, the Lamb, do they paint?

13. **Challenge question**. The religious life of God's Old Testament people revolved around the work of the priests. Aaron and his sons were the first priests God chose (Exodus 28:1).

a. Skim Leviticus 1:1–5; 2:1–2; 3:1–2; 4:27–31; and 5:14–16. What was the role of God's Old Testament priests?

b. God had particular rules for His priests. Skim Leviticus 21. Focus on verse 17. Why did God require that His priests be without defect? (See Hebrews 9:13–14.)

c. While Aaron and God's other Old Testament priests were to typify Christ's perfection, these Old Testament priests were still sinners. On the Day of Atonement, the priests were required to offer sacrifices for their own sins (Leviticus 16:17). None of the animal sacrifices could take away sins. A *perfect* sacrifice offered by a *perfect* priest was needed. Read Hebrews 7:23–28. What three or four differences set Jesus' priesthood apart from the Old Testament priesthood?

14. How do the pictures of Jesus as shepherd and priest unify the message of the Scriptures?

Day 5 • Read Hebrews 13:8

15. Consider carefully the truth presented in today's Scripture reading.

a. What does this verse tell you about Jesus, your Savior?

b. What does it tell you about the message of the Scriptures?

16. Suppose someone said to you, "I tried reading the Bible once. It seemed like page after page of random stories. It might have been important to people long ago, but I see no meaning for me today." Based on your study this week, how would you answer?

Enrichment Magazine

IN THIS ISSUE …

The Bible and Other "Holy Books" 3

Get the Big Picture 5

The Dead Sea Scrolls 10

Martin Luther and the Art of Bible Translation 12

God's Wonderful Word … 14

Context, Not Pretext! 15

Can It Be Poetry If It Doesn't Rhyme? 18

Facts about the Bible to Help You Witness 19

Bible Reading Guides (Reproducible) 20

When God Shows Up 22

Bible Study Helps 24

Read through the Bible in a Year 26

How We Got Our Bible 30

A Prayer Before Reading the Scripture 32

Cover illustration: Tom Dineen
Graphic design: Karen Pauls
Photography : Jack Hazut
1–stork; 10–Dead Sea; 15–Jerusalem;
25–Jordan River, prayer shawl; 30–writing the Torah, Torah displayed in a celebration
Illustration: Art Kirchoff; 12–Wartburg Castle

TO THE DIRECTOR

This student folder contains nine study leaflets and the enrichment magazine. Remove the staples and distribute the leaflets as indicated in the leaders guide. This magazine should be distributed at the first session for use throughout the course.

3558 S. Jefferson Ave., St. Louis, Mo 63118-3968
1-800-325-3040 • cph.org

Edited by Jane L. Fryar

This publication may be available in Braille, in large print, or on cassette tape for the visually impaired. Please allow 8 to 12 weeks for delivery. Write to Lutheran Braille Workers, P.O. Box 5000, Yucaipa, CA 92399; call toll-free 1-800-925-6092; or visit the website: LBWinc.org.

Manufactured in the U.S.A.

9 10 11 12 13 27 26 25 24 23

Cover illustration concept: Jeremiah 23:28–29 uses three figures of speech for God's Word—grain, fire, hammer. The Law of God acts as a hammer, crushing hardened hearts and leading people to repentance. Like fire, the divine Law ultimately tests the quality of every person's work (1 Cor. 3:13). Just as Jesus Himself is the Bread of Life, so His Word is grain—feeding and nourishing our spiritual lives. This grain has nothing in common with the chaff of false teachers. The Gospel empowers God's people to believe and obey Him. The art designed for this LifeLight course incorporates all three of these word pictures.

The Scriptures of Islam

The religion known as Islam today boasts of nearly one billion followers. Theoretically Islam accepts both the Old and New Testaments. But they have added another "revelation." They believe that God revealed the Qur'an (Koran) to Muhammad (A.D. 570–632). While Muslims honor the Bible as a revelation from God, the Qur'an is supposed to be God's final word to His human creatures. Unfortunately, they cannot have it both ways. One cannot respect the Bible as a divine book and at the same time accept another revelation that continually contradicts it. This is just the dilemma in which Muhammad's followers are entangled. Centuries ago, the reformer Martin Luther noted some of the basic conflicts between the Qur'an and the Bible:

> Muhammad denies that Christ is the Son of God, denies that He died for our sins, denies that He arose again to bring us to life, denies that through faith in Him our sins are forgiven and we are justified, denies that He will come as the Judge of the living and the dead—though he does believe in a resurrection of the dead and a day of judgment—denies the Holy Spirit, and denies His gifts. By these and similar articles the conscience must be fortified against the rites of Muhammad. By these means his Alcoran [Qur'an] must be refuted.

Muslim scholars have tried various ways to wiggle out of this bind. One of the more often used justifications is to claim that the Bible was changed after Muhammad's time in order to make it contradict the Qur'an. Yet the existence of numerous copies of the Scriptures predating Muhammad attest to the fact that Scripture has not been changed over the years.

I BELIEVE the Bible is the best gift God has ever given to man. All the good from the Savior of the world is communicated to us through this book.

Abraham Lincoln

The Bible and Other "Holy Books"

The Bible is not the only book held sacred by adherents worldwide. There are many others, including Islam's Qur'an (Koran) as well as the scriptures of the Hindus, Baha'is, Mormons, and Christian Scientists.

People wonder, "How can I tell which one to trust?" Some believe that all such books contain religious truth, and which one we follow is simply a matter of one's upbringing or personal preference. Others contend that this or that religious book has superseded the Bible and now replaces it. Still others believe all religious scriptures are misleading, and we should rely on human reason, not on some so-called divine revelation.

What can the Christian say to all this? We rightly speak of the Bible as the "Book of books," that is, the Book excelling all others. But just what are the differences between the Bible and the sacred books of other religions? What sets it apart?

There are numerous differences, including the Bible's surpassing greatness as literature. Unlike any other ancient book, the Bible has a never-ending freshness about it and a power that continues to change lives and uplift entire nations. The Bible comforts, encourages, and inspires as no other book. But of all the distinctions, two separate the Bible from every other scripture in such a way as to make it tower above them as an Everest among foothills.

First, the Bible is grounded in history. For an example of what this means, we turn to the sacred writings of the Orient. Among them are the Hindu Upanishads, written between 800 and 400 B.C. These scriptures include thoughts like this:

> *O Lord, let me come unto thee and come thou unto me, O Lord. In thy waters, O my Lord, may I wash my sins away.*

Here we have a moving request for peace and forgiveness, for closeness to God. It sounds almost like a Christian prayer, except that it has no awareness of the God who entered this world as its Savior and who said, "No one comes to the Father except through Me" (John 14:6). Consequently, the Hindu prayer for forgiveness carries no assurance that it will be answered. For, unlike the Bible, other "sacred books" have nothing solid on which to rest their hopes, speculations, wishes, and prayers.

In contrast to this, the Bible rests on the fulfillment of prophecy, particularly on the life, death, and resurrection of the Savior whom God had promised to send. The Bible offers these facts as the demonstration of God's faithfulness, love, and power. In other words, while many "holy books" might soar into lofty philosophical speculations, only the Bible anchors its lofty claims. It anchors them to miraculous, yet historical events and specifically to Jesus Christ. This is unique among religious books.

Other religious books, of course, do recognize the Bible as special. They claim to honor it and to build on it. Here we find Islam, second only to Christianity in numbers of adherents, as well as religions such as Mormonism, Christian Science, and Bahaism. Islam adds the Qur'an to the Bible. Mormonism adds *The Book of Mormon* and other writings of Joseph Smith. Christian Science adds Mary Baker Eddy's *Science and Health with Keys to the Scriptures*. The Baha'is add the sacred books of other religions as well as the writings of the Baha'i prophets Baha' Allah and Abdul Baha.

Since these religions acknowledge the Bible, we might at least expect them to come to terms with its fundamental teachings. Sadly, this is something they all fail to do. Especially do they fail to come to terms with the Bible's central theme—salvation by grace through faith in the Savior, Jesus Christ.

And that brings us to the second, and most important, distinction. Only the Bible teaches that salvation is a free gift of God's grace through faith in Jesus. Every other "holy book" teaches the natural religion of sinful, fallen human beings—that we must save ourselves. The Bible demonstrates that it is impossible for sinful people to please the just and holy God. The equation is simple: believe the Bible and rely on Jesus or believe any other "holy book" and be thrown back on the same old pattern of trying to save yourself by doing the impossible.

Many in our culture hold the notion that the very idea of "divine revelation" is behind the times, that with our scientific way of discovering truth we need nothing but our own intellect. This, too, is but another variation of the do-it-yourself approach to religion. When it comes to understanding the meaning of life, our origins and destiny, human reason is extremely limited. We can guess, but in guessing we enjoy no certainty. That is why God declares:

> *For it is written: "I will destroy the wisdom of the wise; the intelligence of the intelligent I will frustrate." Where is the wise man? Where is the scholar? Where is the philosopher of this age? Has not God made foolish the wisdom of the world? (1 Corinthians 1:19–20).*

Where, then, can certainty, meaning, and absolute truth be found? As the philosopher Ludwig Wittgenstein recognized, "The sense of the world must lie outside the world." In other words, the only way we can ever get a proper picture of life in this world is if we could somehow step outside it and see the entire picture. Of course, no human being is able to do this. God, however, can. He can see eternal truths which lie outside the grasp of our limited reason. If He chooses to do so, He can reveal to us the truth we could never discover on our own. That is exactly what the Bible does.

Get the Big Picture

Suppose someone from Europe wants to visit North America, wants to spend two weeks getting to know firsthand what our lives and culture are like. Before such a person gets on an airplane headed for Paducah, Kentucky, he or she would be well-advised to get an overview of North American history and geography. Knowing that Canada, the United States, and Mexico share space on the continent would be helpful. Understanding the location of the Great Lakes and the Rocky Mountains would be important. Learning some basic words and phrases in English, French, and Spanish would be wise.

As we approach the Bible, we likewise do well to have a general idea of its overall structures, arrangement, and vocabulary. Here are some facts you may find helpful, whether you are opening your Bible for the first time or reading it through for the 50th.

- The Bible is not really a book but a *library* of 66 individual books, some as long as 150 chapters and some short enough to be a tract or pamphlet.
- The two main divisions of the Bible are the Old Testament—dealing with the history of God's people before Jesus' birth, and the New Testament—dealing with Jesus' life, death, resurrection, ascension, and His work through His church beginning in the first century and continuing in His people still today.
- The 66 Bible books employ different genres—historical narrative, poetry, parables, proverbs, letters, and an almost surrealistic writing style known as "apocalyptic." Discerning a book's style is of critical importance in understanding its message.

The Old Testament

The ancient Jews divided the Hebrew Scriptures—the part we know as the Old Testament—into three main sections—the Law, the Prophets, and the Writings. The first five books of the Bible are historical narrative with some poetry sprinkled in. They are called the *Books of Moses,* since he authored the text. Another name is *Pentateuch,* a Greek term meaning "five volumes." Yet another is the *Law* or *Torah,* the Hebrew designation for law, since several of these books tell about the giving of the Law at Mt. Sinai. People sometimes get the mistaken impression that the Torah contains only law. In fact, *all* Scripture contains both Law—exposing our sin, and Gospel—promising God's love and forgiveness.

The next nine books are also mostly historical narrative and cover the history of Abraham's descendants from 1400 B.C. to the time the Babylonians invaded Palestine and led the people into exile in 586 B.C. Joshua, Samson, Gideon, David, Solomon, Ahab, Hezekiah, Sennacherib—believers and pagans, saints and sinners—all walk across these pages and into the

mists of time, by grace fulfilling God's purposes in their generations. After Babylon fell to the Persians, the Jews were allowed to return to their homeland and rebuild the city of Jerusalem. The books of Ezra, Nehemiah, and Esther recount some of the history of this time.

While as much as one-third of the Old Testament is poetical in form, five books (Job, Psalms, Proverbs, Ecclesiastes, Song of Solomon) are specifically known as the poetic books. These are the "Writings" of the Old Testament. At times these books are also referred to as wisdom literature. They emphasize how we are to live, and they offer godly wisdom concerning some of life's most complex problems.

The "Prophets" make up the remainder of the Old Testament books. Isaiah, Jeremiah (including the brief book of Lamentations also written by Jeremiah), Ezekiel, and Daniel are known as the major prophets, the rest being known as the minor prophets. (The terms *major* and *minor* refer not to the importance of their message, but only to the length of their books.) The prophets were the great Old Testament preachers. Through them God spoke. Through many of them, He wrote. And in them we see the awesome power of God's Word. The Lord says, "Is not My Word like fire ...and like a hammer that breaks a rock in pieces?" (Jeremiah 23:29). The prophets also foresaw the future. They foretold God's judgment upon His apostate people and upon the heathen nations. Most important, they proclaimed the Savior who was to come.

The New Testament

The life of Jesus Christ is the focal point of all history. He came to destroy the power of sin, death, and the devil. He came to win forgiveness and eternal life for our fallen race. Having accomplished all this, He ascended to heaven with the promise to return as Judge of the living and the dead.

The gospels, the first four books of the New Testament, recount these momentous events. The word *gospel* means "Good News," and the writers of these books bear the title *evangelist,* a Greek word meaning "one who brings good news."

The first three gospels are called "synoptic." The term refers to the fact that the writers' approaches are similar in many respects, and they often record the same events. Yet within that similarity, each writer has his own distinct emphasis. All four gospels emphasize Christ's suffering and death. As one theologian put it, they are "passion narratives with extended introductions."

While none of these books names its author, from earliest times Christians have known who the sacred writers were: Matthew, Mark, Luke, John.

The book of Acts then takes up where the gospels leave off. Written by Luke, this book recounts the history of the early church. Like ripples from a stone cast into the water, we see the Good News moving out in ever widening circles. By the final chapter of Acts, the Gospel has reached Rome itself, in those days the world's capital and its greatest city.

Of the New Testament's 27 books, 21 are epistles or letters. And of those, 13 come from the hand of the apostle Paul. Paul addressed most of his letters to congregations, the rest to individual Christians. The letters are not arranged in the order they were written. Romans comes first, because it is considered his most important letter. Martin Luther called this letter "the chief part of the New Testament and the purest Gospel." Paul's life and letters remind us of God's grace to sinners. Like Paul who called himself, "the least of the apostles," we, too, want to live for our Savior. We know that, for "us to live is Christ and to die is gain" (Philippians 1:21).

While Paul directed his letters to congregations and individual Christians, most of the other New Testament letters are not addressed to specific congregations or people. They are known as the "general letters" or catholic epistles, that is, intended for the church at large. Although different men wrote these books, the general letters harmoniously direct us to Jesus.

Except for Hebrews, whose author is unnamed, the general letters are named for their writers. The first four encourage Christians in faith and good works: Hebrews; James; 1 and 2 Peter. The last four focus on love and truth: 1, 2, and 3 John; Jude.

Revelation, the last book of the Bible, was probably written about A.D. 95, during a time when the early church faced persecution for not worshiping the Roman emperor. The apostle John (who also wrote one of the gospels and three epistles) wrote to comfort those Christians, and believers of all times. Moreover, the book warns against succumbing to Satan's temptations and falling away from the faith.

Revelation is a distinct type of literature known as "apocalyptic," a kind of writing that is highly symbolic. For example, stars represent angels, and lampstands are churches. The Revelation frequently uses numbers, especially the number seven, which symbolizes completeness.

The book's last chapter forms a magnificent conclusion to the story of salvation. Here John brings us full circle from the opening three chapters of Genesis, as he shows us paradise restored—with its river of life and tree of life. Here we have Jesus' wonderful promise, "Behold, I am coming soon! Blessed is he who keeps the words of the prophecy in this book" (22:7). And here we join in the prayer of Christians of all times and places, "Amen. Come, Lord Jesus" (22:20).

What about the Aztecs?

The historical books of the Old Testament focus most of their attention on one small nation. They relate the story of God's chosen people from Abraham through the time Israel entered the Promised Land as nomadic tribes under Joshua. After several centuries Israel became a monarchy, rose to glory under kings David and Solomon, split into two rival kingdoms (Israel and Judah), and fell into ruin. By the end of the Old Testament era, only a remnant of the nation remained. From that remnant, the Savior of the world would come.

Knowing what we today know about world history, we may be inclined to question this focus. "Didn't God care about the Incas of Central America?" we may wonder. "Didn't He take the ancient Chinese civilization into account? Why such a narrow focus on so few people, relatively speaking?" we may ask. The answer is that the Bible is not designed to be a book on world history. God did not inspire it so that we could answer the questions raised by speculation and curiosity. Rather, Scripture serves one, unique purpose. By it our Lord intends that we become "wise unto salvation" (2 Timothy 3:15 KJV). Israel's history is the history of the salvation God prepared for us in Jesus Christ. Not even all of Israel's ancient history appears in Scripture. The Holy Spirit focuses on God's specific and gracious work in preserving the line of Abraham and David from which He had promised to bring our Savior, His Promised Messiah.

The Books of the Bible

Old Testament

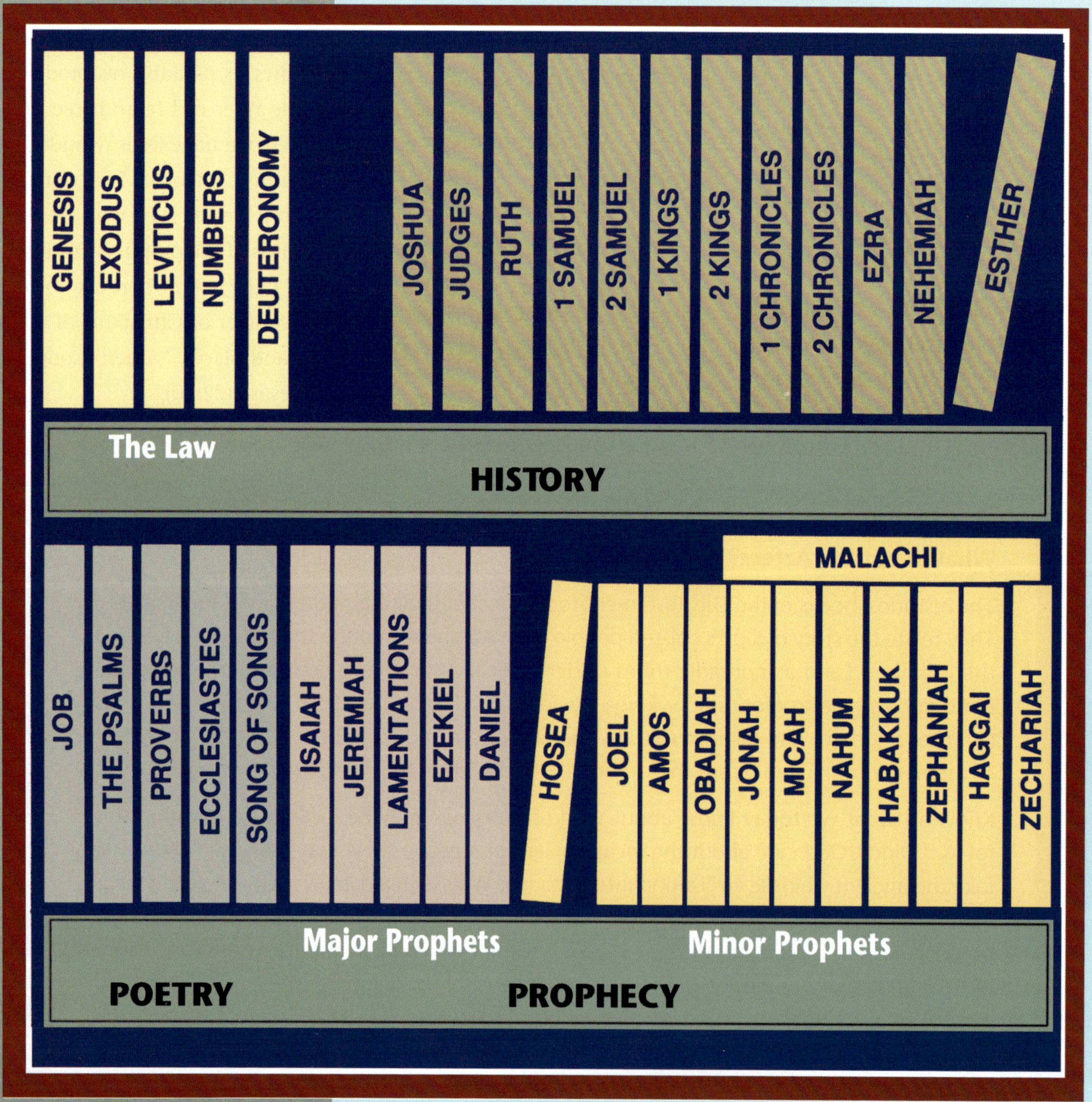

New Testament

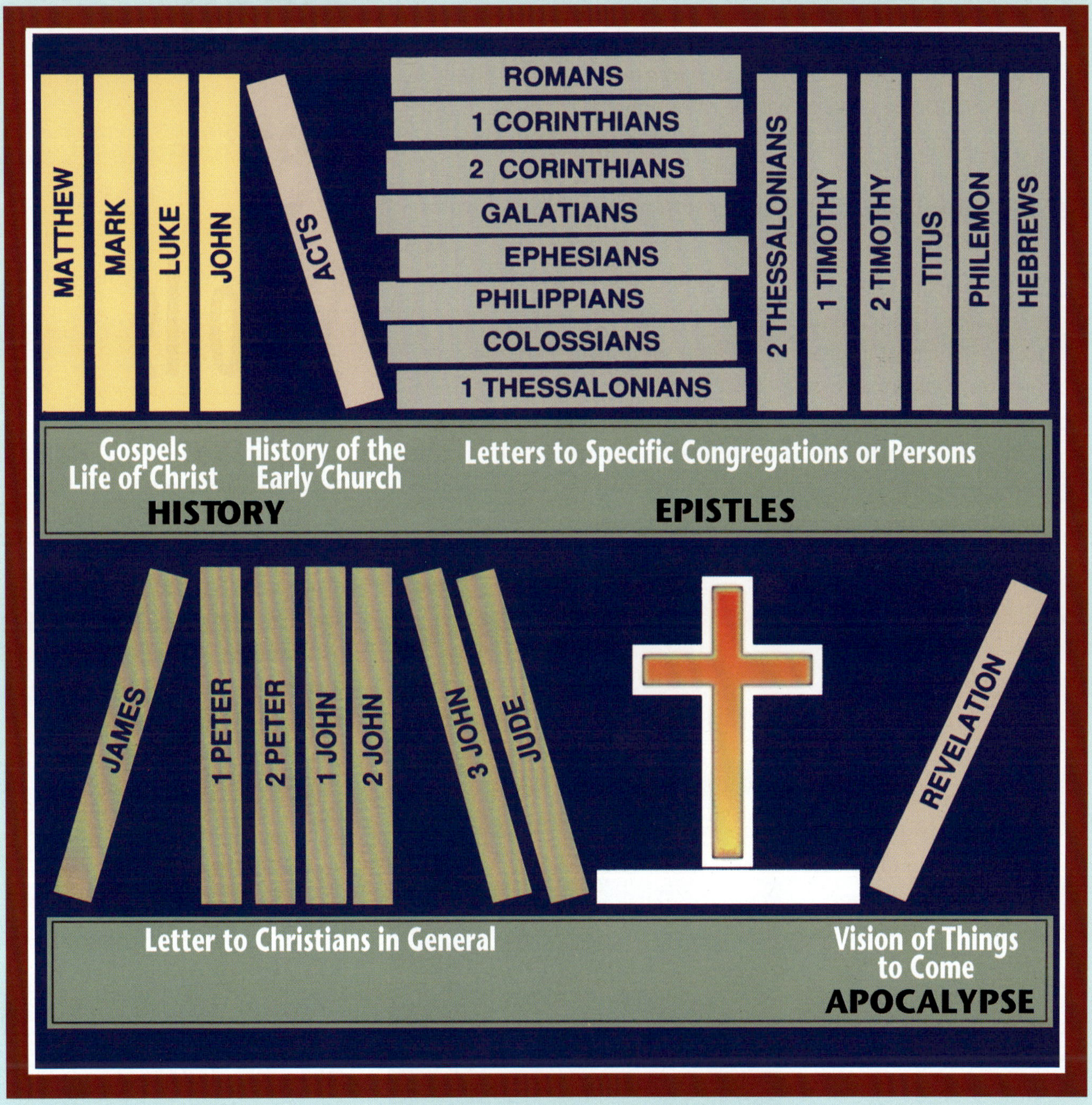

The Essene Sect

Along the northwestern coast of the Dead Sea lies a promontory barren of trees, of grass, of shrubs—of all vegetation. The unforgiving sun has baked the sand for centuries. But here, 200 or so years before Christ, a small community of Jews settled, a strict sect whose members called themselves "the Holy Ones." We know them as the Essenes.

This band of dissenters left Jerusalem in protest against the worldly ways their fellow Jews had adopted. They built a quite elaborate enclave where they prayed, meditated, and took frequent ritual baths in an effort to purify themselves for the coming of the Messiah. To accommodate these "baptisms," their enclave included a system of pools and waterfalls fed by a broad aqueduct.

Some scholars believe that John the Baptizer grew up among the Essenes. John's mother, Elizabeth, and his father, Zechariah, were well along in years when John was born. If the boy was orphaned at an early age, it is possible the Essenes—celibate themselves—took him in. If this is so, then perhaps his knowledge of the Scriptures, his preference for preaching in the wilderness, his rather wild appearance, and the baptism that became his hallmark were all part of the legacy of the Essenes.

This unique Essene settlement, known as Khirbat Qumran or "Enclave of the Essenes," has left us a second, more certain legacy. The Essenes—or some of them at least—were scribes who spent their days copying Old Testament texts on long leather scrolls—the Dead Sea scrolls found nearly two millennia later by a Bedouin shepherd boy.

The Dead Sea Scrolls

In 1947, a Bedouin shepherd boy discovered the first of the now-famous scrolls in one of the caves near the northwest end of the Dead Sea, less than 20 miles from Jerusalem. The find was soon recognized as the greatest manuscript discovery in modern times.

It seems likely that the Essenes put the scrolls in caves in order to hide them from the Roman armies, who in A.D. 68 passed through the area as they swept down on Jerusalem to crush a Jewish revolt. (The temple in Jerusalem was destroyed in A.D. 70.) Stored in earthenware jars, the scrolls remained in the desert caves for some 19 centuries.

These scrolls contain the oldest known copies of the Old Testament Scriptures. More than that, they represent a wealth of other material as well. They include every book of the Old Testament, except Esther, along with numerous other documents dating from approximately 140 B.C. to A.D. 68. Scrolls and fragments of scrolls have been found in 11 different caves. Among the materials from Cave 1 (the site of the original discovery) was a complete scroll of the book of Isaiah, dating from before 100 B.C., written on leather, and 24' long. Cave 4 contained the richest repository of materials, with some 15,000 fragments representing about 500 different documents!

> The Bible is no mere book, but a Living Creature, with a power that conquers all who oppose it.
>
> Napoleon Bonaparte

Fifty years after their discovery, the scrolls continue to make news. The popular press has tended to focus on controversies among scholars concerning the scrolls, often hinting that the scrolls contained secrets that might dramatically change our ideas about the origins of the Christian faith or the true contents of the Old Testament.

The scrolls are, in fact, important—for two main reasons. First, they greatly enrich our knowledge of ancient times. They show, for example, how the Qumran community followed the legalistic teachings of someone known as the "Teacher of Righteousness" and the importance they placed on outward purity. Far from changing our ideas about Jesus, the scrolls only confirm His uniqueness. Jesus' message of forgiveness and love stands in sharp contrast to the exclusive and legalistic message of the Essenes.

Second, the Dead Sea scrolls provide understanding of how carefully the Old Testament text was transmitted. These scrolls are 1,000 years older than any previously oldest known copies of the Hebrew Scriptures. And yet they attest to the faithfulness of the Holy Spirit in preserving His Word for us. None of the fragments in any way disproves or calls into question any essential doctrine of the faith.

Martin Luther
and the Art of Bible Translation

In 1522, Martin Luther lived in virtual exile in the Wartburg castle. The Pope had issued what amounted to a death warrant on the Reformer. While circumstances looked bleak, the Lord had them well in hand. In the amazing span of only 11 weeks, Luther translated the entire Greek New Testament into German. (His Old Testament translation was completed in Wittenberg in 1534 with the help of other Reformation scholars.)

Martin Luther's translation of the Bible into the German language has been called the crowning achievement of his life's work. It is still read in Germany today. Luther's was not the first translation of the Bible into German, but it was the most excellent and influential. The common people could now read the Word of God in their own language. Luther's German translation gave impetus to other translators, particularly to those who translated the Bible into English. Because Luther's work as a translator was so influential, we do well to consider some of what he had to say about Bible translation. Many in Luther's day, as in our own, despised the fact that they had the Word of God in their own language. May we never be numbered with them! Rather, may the Holy Spirit move us to search the Word and to make it a part of our lives.

The Balance between a Literal and a Readable Translation

What purpose does it serve unnecessarily to abide by the words so rigidly and strictly that people can get no sense out of them? Whoever would speak German must not use Hebrew idioms; but if he understands the Hebrew writer, he must see to it that he grasps his meaning and must think: Now let me see. How does a German speak in this case? When he has the German words that serve the purpose, then let him dismiss the Hebrew words and freely express the sense in the best German he is capable of using.

(*What Luther Says,* 1:105–106)

Hard Work Makes for Easy Reading

I have constantly striven to produce a pure and clear German in translating; and it often happened that for two or three or four weeks we sought and asked for a single word and at times did not find it even then. Such was our labor while translating Job that … I could at times scarcely finish three lines in four days. To be sure, now that it is done into German and is completed, anyone can read and criticize it. … It is easy plowing when the field is cleaned up; but rooting up the woods and the stumps and preparing the field—that is the job no one wants to tackle.

(*What Luther Says,* 1:106)

Christ's Love As Luther's Motivator

I have had such trouble with translating! No one would have persuaded me by favors or gold to translate a book had I not done it for the sake of my Lord Christ. …

(*What Luther Says,* 1:107)

The Difficulty of Translation

Translating is certainly not everybody's business, as the mad saints imagine. It requires a genuinely pious, faithful, diligent, God-fearing, experienced, practiced heart. Therefore I hold that a false Christian … is unable to give a faithful translation.

(*What Luther Says,* 1:105)

God's Wonderful Word Is All We Need for Faith and Life Eternal!

God's Word Is:

Authoritative: The Word creates, sustains, and guides faith. Matt. 24:35; Lk. 4:32–36, 24:44; Jn. 10:35, 12:48; 1 Cor. 1:18, 14:37; 1 Thes. 2:13; 2 Tim. 3:16; 2 Pet. 1:21

Sufficient: Scripture teaches everything necessary for faith. Deut. 4:2; Josh. 1:7–8; Ps. 19:7; Matt. 5:17; Mk. 16:20; Jn. 8:12–20, 17:17, 20:31; Acts 20:32; Rom. 1:16–17, 10:17, 16:17; 1 Cor. 1:21; Eph. 1:13; 1 Tim. 6:3–5; Rev. 22:18–19

Clear: Scripture illuminates itself. Ps. 19:7–8, 119:105, 130; Matt. 11:25; Jn. 5:39; Acts 17:11; 2 Cor. 1:19–20, 4:3–6; 2 Tim. 3:15; 2 Pet. 1:19; 1 Jn. 2:12–13

Efficacious: The Word is living. It accomplishes that which it commands. Deut. 8:3; Is. 55:10–11; Lam. 2:17; Lk. 8:11–15; Jn. 6:63; Acts 6:7, 12:24, 19:20; Rom. 10:17; 1 Cor. 1:21, 2:4–5; 2 Cor. 4:6; Phil. 2:16; 1 Thes. 2:13; Jam. 1:21; 1 Pet. 1:23, 2:2; 1 Jn. 1:1–2

The chart below is not meant to be critical. Rather it simply shows what various groups believe and teach regarding God's Word, based on their own published works.

Roman Catholic	Orthodox	Liberal	Reformed	Lutheran	Mormon Jehovah's Witness
According to its latest catechism, 1992, the Roman Catholic Church "does not derive her certainty about all revealed truths from Scriptures alone. Both Scripture and tradition must be accepted and honored with equal sentiments of devotion and reverence." Church councils and papal decrees have as much, or more, authority than the Bible. No one can understand Scripture without interpretation of the church.	Holy Scripture is not considered the final and complete source of doctrine. "Sacred tradition" must also determine doctrine. The church in her ecumenical councils is the authentic and infallible interpreter of divine revelation as contained in Scriptures and "sacred tradition."	The Bible is not the Word of God. It is full of errors, even in theology, and must be studied *historically-critically,* like all other secular writings. Its truth is not literal, but symbolic, like parables.	Scripture is the highest authority and source of doctrine and life. Word of God and Holy Spirit can be separated, therefore, the Word is not always "spirit and life," as taught in John 6:63. Helvetic Confession: "God teaches us outwardly in His Word through ministers, but inwardly He leads the hearts of His elect to faith through the Holy Spirit."	Scripture is the highest source and authority for faith and life. The Bible is above all the book of Christ and the Gospel, calling for faith and trust. Word and Spirit are never separate. Through His **living** Word, God justifies and sanctifies man. God's Word is clear, and accomplishes that which it commands.	Book of Mormon is of equal authority with the Bible. Mormons deny the deity of Christ and are a non-Christian sect. Jehovah's Witnesses mistranslate and distort John 1:1, and thereby deny Christ's deity. They are a non-Christian sect.

Context, Not Pretext!

Sometimes faithful Christians find themselves grieved by cynics who scoff, "You can make the Bible prove anything." Or, "That's *your* interpretation." By this, they mean to raise doubt about any truths drawn from Scripture.

So how about it? *Can* one "make the Bible prove anything"? Legitimately? No. Not any more than we can make Shakespeare's *Othello* "prove anything." Of course, one can do ridiculous exercises like stringing every fifth word of the manuscript together and thus forming a quote that may seem to allude to Einstein's general theory of relativity or Marilyn Monroe's place in entertainment history. But almost anyone recognizes that this is not a legitimate method of interpretation.

Then what is? How can any rational person—true believer or skeptic—approach the text of Scripture to determine what it truly says? Whole books have been written to answer those questions. But we can summarize one of the most important keys in a single word: *context.*

The true meaning of a text can be gained only by studying the words, phrases, or passages (larger sections of text) in their setting—in relation to what comes before and follows after.

Unless we read a text in context we can easily use it as a pretext to support our own pet theories or misguided opinions. We do violence to what the Holy Spirit intends to teach us unless we consider the context.

But what is a "context"? Think of that in terms of the diagram on page 17. Each text of Scripture is surrounded by four circles of context.

We read all Scripture in the context of Calvary.

First, a given verse is ringed by verses that precede and follow it. Perhaps your Bible divides chapters into paragraphs. When we want to know the meaning of a verse, we need to study the paragraph in which it is set and then the chapter in which it is found. We ask ourselves, "How does this verse fit in with its setting? How does it advance the main point the author is making?"

Second, any interpretation needs to take into account the entire book or letter in which a text appears. This setting carries enormous weight in interpreting a given verse or passage. For instance, in Romans 1–2 the apostle Paul delivers a stinging indictment of all humanity. A person who read only this indictment could walk away certain that God hates His human creatures or that He wants us to live in shame and fear. But in the context of the entire letter, we see that nothing could be farther from the truth. Romans is a ringing affirmation of God's love for His fallen creatures. It promises all who are in Christ Jesus forgiveness and freedom from condemnation.

Third, a text needs to be considered in light of all the books written by the same human author. For example, a full understanding of Exodus 20, the giving of the Law on Mount Sinai, is impossible without a knowledge of Genesis 3, Genesis 15, Exodus 19, and probably also the entire system of sacrifice described in Leviticus, especially the Day of Atonement from chapter 16—all these written by Moses. Can a reader grasp the Ten Commandments given on Sinai without knowing other things Moses wrote about the relationship between a holy God and sinful people? Yes, but only partially. From Exodus 20 alone, outside the context of the two covenants Moses describes (Abraham's covenant and the covenant of Sinai), a reader can easily come away with a mistaken notion about the purposes for which the Lord gave His Law.

This brings us to the fourth circle of context—the entirety of Scripture. We cannot understand Mount Calvary without a grasp of Mount Sinai—and vice versa. The themes of Scripture, particularly the foundational truth of salvation by grace through faith for Jesus' sake, must inform our approach to any passage. We read all Scripture in the context of Calvary and of Christ's open tomb.

An old story illustrates the importance of interpreting texts in context. Supposedly a young man had dated every girl in his college class. He saw positive qualities in them all and debated with himself about which girl he would like to marry. Troubled and indecisive, he finally closed his eyes, opened his Bible (King James Version), and pointed to a verse at random. When he opened his eyes, he saw these words, "Ye have need of patience." (Hebrews 10:36 KJV). Whereupon he ran out to the campus snack bar and proposed—to Patience.

Circles of Context

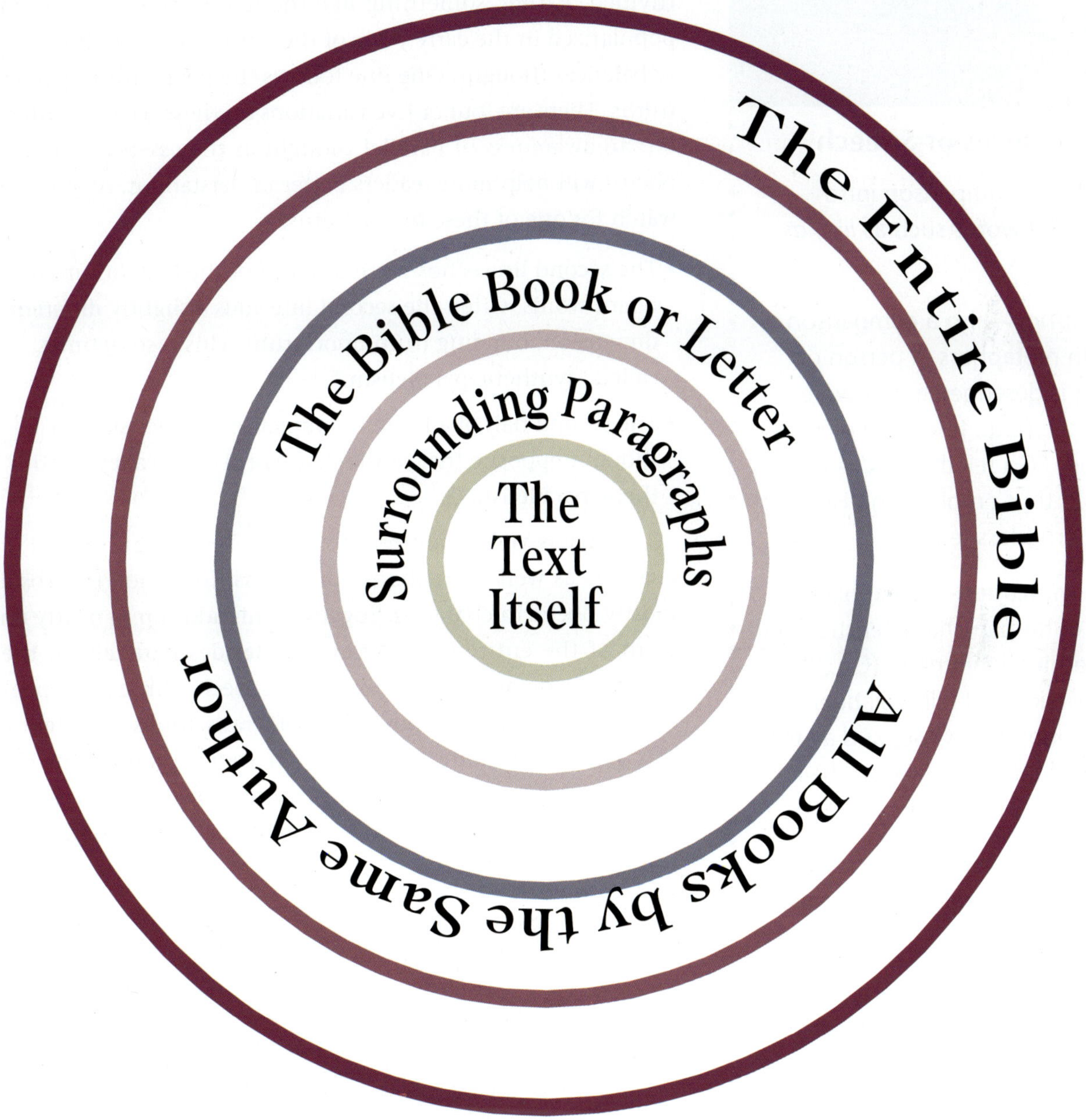

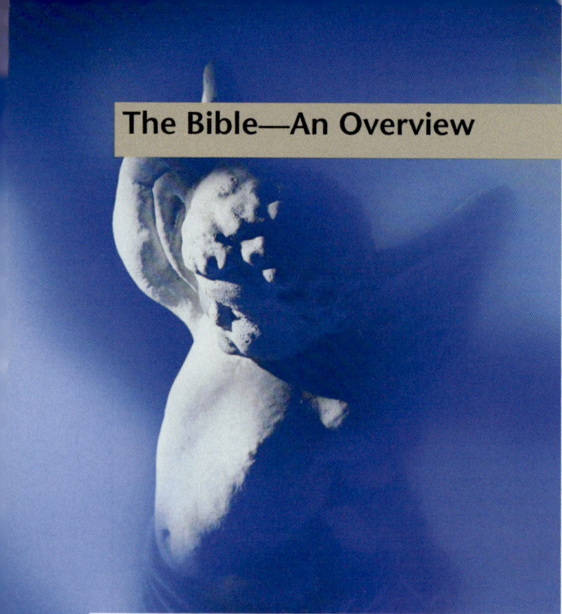

Can It Be Poetry If It Doesn't Rhyme?

From the doggerel that appears as graffiti on the school child's notebook to the sonnets of Shakespeare, most of the poetry we have come to know uses fairly strict meter and rhyming words at the ends of lines. Hebrew poetry—the poetry of the Old Testament—does not do this. Not even the original Hebrew rhymed. Rather, something like the free verse e. e. cummings popularized in the early years of the 20th century, Hebrew poetry balances thought. One line follows the next, creating parallel truths. There are four or five variations on these parallel patterns, but an awareness of parallel thought as the essence of Hebrew poetry will help most readers better understand it. As you read, watch for one of these two patterns:

- The second line echos the main idea of the first, but in different words. Often the second line adds a slightly different dimension, building truth upon truth. This is sometimes called "synthetic parallelism."
- The second half of a Hebrew couplet sometimes states a thought opposite that of the first half. This is called "antithetic parallelism."

Poetry is very common in the Old Testament. Almost 150 chapters as well as the books of Psalms, Job, and Proverbs are mostly poetic in character. Together, this adds up to nearly one-third of the entire Old Testament! Besides parallelism, these chapters generally use the figures of speech common to poetry in every language. In times past, Bible translations often ignored this. Poetry looked the same way as narrative prose on the page. Most contemporary English translations, however, now do print the poetry of Scripture in a kind of free verse format to show that it is poetry.

Hebrew poetry employs a balance of thought and rhythm.

Figures of Speech

Simile—a comparison introduced by words such as *like, as,* or *than.*

Metaphor—also a comparison, but in metaphors, a person or thing is described as if it were another. (E.g., Jesus said of King Herod, "Go tell that fox"—Luke 13:32, thus emphasizing Herod's crafty ruthlessness.)

Personification—the application of human characteristics to something inanimate. (E.g., "The mountains and hills will burst into song before You, and all the trees of the field will clap their hands"—Isaiah 55:12.)

Hyperbole—an exaggeration for effect, not meant to be taken literally.

Interrogation—a means of emphasizing a truth by asking a question; a rhetorical question. See Romans 8:31–32.

FACTS about the Bible to Help You Witness

Often someone will sarcastically remark concerning the Bible, "You can't trust the Bible. It's full or errors." The fact is, however, that we can trust the Holy Scriptures. How reliable are the copies we have? We can appreciate the reliability of the New Testament if we compare it to textual material from other works of roughly the same time period. Note in each case the time span that separates the original work from the earliest copy as you study the chart below.

Author	When Written	Earliest Copy	Time Span	Number of Copies
Pliny the Younger	A.D. 61–113	850 A.D.	750 yrs.	7
Caesar	100–44 B.C.	900 A.D.	1,000 yrs.	10
Plato	427–347 B.C.	900 A.D.	1,200 yrs.	7
Aristotle	384–322 B.C.	1100 A.D.	1,400 yrs.	37
Sophocles	496–406 B.C.	1000 A.D.	1,400 yrs.	193
Euripedes	480–406 B.C.	1100 A.D.	1,500 yrs.	9
Catallus	54 B.C.	1550 A.D.	1,600 yrs.	3
New Testament	A.D. 48 (Mark)	130 A.D.	80 yrs.	24,630 (N.T.)

Bible Reading Guides (Reproducible)

As you develop a personal plan of Bible study, feel free to duplicate the worksheets below. Use a new one each time you begin your study of a given text. Chose the worksheet designed for the kind of Biblical literature you will be studying.

> If some passage is obscure I consider whether it treats of grace or of Law, whether wrath or the forgiveness of sin [is contained in it], and with which of these it agrees better. By this procedure I have often understood the most obscure of passages. Either the Law or Gospel has made them meaningful, for God divides His teaching into Law and Gospel.
>
> Martin Luther

Old Testament Narrative

a. Where is God's care and preservation of His people evident in this text?

b. What hints, if any, do you see of God's future deliverance in Jesus, the Savior?

c. Where does God's Law confront you in this passage? In other words, where do you see your need, sins, or failures?

d. Where in this passage do you see the Gospel—God's forgiveness, provision, and strength for you?

Psalms or Other Old Testament Poetry

a. What descriptions, comparisons, or contrasts stand out for you in this reading?

b. Where do you see Jesus in this reading?

c. Is this reading a prayer? If so, about what or for what is the writer praying?

d. What situations or events in your own life have caused you to have similar thoughts or to pray a prayer similar to this one?

New Testament Narrative

a. Briefly summarize Jesus' actions in this text.

b. What does the text reveal to you about Jesus?

c. What does the text reveal to you about yourself?

d. Where is God's grace evident in this text?

When God Shows Up

When God strides onto the scene, everything changes. Adam and Eve, hiding in the bushes of Eden, knew that. It's why they quivered in fear and shame (Genesis 3). The prophet Isaiah knew that. It's why he yearned for the Lord to appear to his beleaguered and sinful people:

Oh, that You would rend the heavens!
That You would come down!
That the mountains might shake at Your presence.
(Isaiah 64:1 NKJV)

Believing Christians know that God has shown up—in Jesus Christ. We also believe that He comes to us each time we open the Holy Scriptures. But what can we expect of Him? What will He do when He comes? Far from being a dry-as-dust intellectual exercise, reading the Scripture touches our hearts in the most profound way we can be touched. When God shows up, He moves us—to repentance and faith.

Law

God may speak words of Law—words that humble and terrify us, words that crush us because they expose our sin, our nakedness before our Creator. Adam and Eve experienced this, as we have just said. For us, as for them, God's Law reveals the depth of our depravity, our moral bankruptcy before our divine Judge. God's Law reveals the sins of thought, word, and deed by which we have offended our Lord. We have not loved Him with our whole heart. We have not loved our neighbors as ourselves. We have done the evil He forbids. We have not done the good He demands. What's worse, we cannot rectify the situation. We cannot change ourselves, no matter how hard we try. In and of ourselves we don't want to obey; we don't even want to try!

We reverence, love, and trust many false gods, gods which cannot help us. Even so, we cling to them with all our hearts. When God's Law forces us to come face-to-face with these facts, we back away in horror. We realize we deserve God's wrath. He could, in perfect justice, fling us from His presence into an eternity apart from Him.

Gospel

But when God shows up, He also wants to speak words of Gospel—Good News—to His repentant people. The Gospel comforts, cheers, and encourages us. It drives the fear from our hearts because it tells us of the great salvation God has prepared for us in His Son, Jesus Christ. The Law makes demands and hurls accusations at us; but the Gospel reveals what God has done for us and soothes our dread. It reveals the truth that the face of our Father is the face of love and pardon. The Gospel is not *do,* but *done.* Not demands, but promises. Not threats, but encouragement.

And the Gospel does even more! Wonder of all wonders, contrary to what our minds clouded by sin would think, the Gospel empowers us to obey the commands of the Law! The Law, you see, has no power—except the power to frighten and to kill. But the Gospel carries with it the power we need to both believe God's love for us and to respond to that love in obedience—true, heartfelt obedience.

Law and Gospel

Understanding this distinction between Law and Gospel is the key to understanding all Scripture. Our study and understanding of any given Bible passage is wrong or incomplete until we have seen God speak Law and Gospel to our hearts through it. How important, then, it is that the Holy Spirit open our minds and our hearts to His truth. Only as the Spirit of God works this in us will we see the true and full meaning of a passage.

As we study Scripture, we can ask ourselves questions like these:

- Does this passage reveal my sin? Does it make demands?
- Does this passage show me my Savior? Does it show me what God has done for me in Christ?

When we identify sin, we simply confess it—that is our Lord's invitation to us. We can rest in the assurance that pardon comes to us from Christ's cross. Then we can look at God's Law in a new light—as a possibility He holds out to us for our joy as His redeemed, righteous people. We no longer *must* obey, we can! We *get to!* His Spirit works both the desire and the power for new obedience in our hearts (Philippians 2:13).

I have known 95 of the world's great men in my time, and of those 87 were followers of the Bible. The Bible is stamped with a specialty of origin, and an immeasurable distance separates it from all competitors.

William E. Gladstone

It is impossible to enslave mentally or socially a Bible-reading people. The principles of the Bible are the groundwork of human freedom.

Horace Greeley

Bible Study Helps

There are numerous books that serve as aids in the study of Scripture. In using them, we should remember that they are not meant as substitutes for reading the Bible itself. Rather, they assist the Christian toward a deeper understanding of God's Word. These helps fall into several basic types.

Atlases

Most Bibles contain several pages of maps. For the person without such a Bible or who is interested in more detailed study of the geography of biblical lands, a Bible atlas is most helpful. Through the use of an atlas we can easily see, for instance, that Palestine was the only land bridge between mighty Egypt and the great kingdoms of the north, Assyria and Babylon. Consequently, the people of Israel often found themselves caught in the middle of colossal struggles for domination of the Middle East. *The Moody Atlas of Bible Lands* by Barry Beitzel is an excellent Bible atlas.

Biblical Archaeology

Archaeology (or archeology) is the study of the remains of past civilizations. The uncovering of ancient cities, buried by centuries of debris and sand, is all part of this science. The excavation of ancient sites in the Middle East in recent decades has shed much light on the activities of people in Bible times. Most archaeology books contain numerous photographs and illustrations which can make history come alive. Among the many fine books in this field are two volumes by Merill F. Unger, one treating each testament.

Commentaries

A commentary is a study of one or more books of the Bible, giving useful insights into the text. Some commentaries furnish in-depth studies of Scripture by making frequent reference to the Hebrew or Greek language of the original. The use of such books can do much to compensate for a lack of formal theological training.

The American Edition of Luther's Works contains 30 volumes of commentaries on large portions of Scripture. These writings by the great Reformer remain some of the most learned and yet readable books of this kind. The People's Bible Commentary series is an excellent companion text for Bible study leaders and for individual use. It weaves together the New International Version of the Bible with in-depth commentaries. The *Concordia Self-Study Commentary* by Walter Roehrs and Martin Franzmann is a concise commentary especially for laypeople. The 12-volume commentary on the New Testament by R. C. H. Lenski is quite comprehensive and would prove a valuable addition to any church library.

Concordances

A concordance is used primarily for two purposes: (1) to find a specific verse or (2) to locate verses that deal with the same topic. For example, if readers looks up the word *love,* they will find a concordance entry something like this:

- 1 Ti 6:10
  For the *l* of money is a root
- 1 Ti 6:11
  faith, *l,* endurance and gentleness.
- Jas 2:5
  He promised those who *l* Him?
- Jas 2:8
  "*L* your neighbor as yourself,"
- 1 Pe 1:8
  you have not seen Him, you *l* Him;

These key sections from specific verses show the various contexts in which the word *love* is used and their location in the Bible.

Some Bibles contain brief concordances that list only the more commonly used words. The *NIV Exhaustive Concordance* by Edward W. Goodrick and John Kohlenberger III includes a numbering system based on Hebrew and Greek words.

Jordan River

Bible Dictionaries

Of all Bible study helps, a good Bible dictionary can prove one of the most useful. This tool lists and explains the names, places, and topics of Scripture. For instance, a reader who wants to know about King David can turn to a good Bible dictionary and find a wealth of information about him.

There are a number of good Bible dictionaries. One of them is the *NIV Compact Dictionary of the Bible* by J. D. Douglas and Merrill C. Tenney, which includes an overview of the Bible along with articles on biblical history and culture. Another is the *Companion Dictionary of the Bible.*

Bible Handbooks

A Bible handbook contains useful introductions to Scripture's 66 books. These introductions include background information (e.g., when a book was written), as well as a brief summary of each book's contents. As you can see, a Bible handbook can help readers set a Bible book in context; often this information is important in interpreting the meaning of passages within the book. Over the years, *Halley's Bible Handbook* has been one of the most popular.

Bible Histories

The glorious events of Scripture have all taken place in history. For this reason, the Christian will be interested in tracing God's saving activities through the ages. Bible histories help satisfy this interest. They often supply additional information on peoples and nations only mentioned in passing in the Holy Scriptures. One of the greatest of Bible historians was Alfred Edersheim whose *Life and Times of Jesus the Messiah* presents a superb picture of the world in which Jesus lived.

Read through the Bible in a Year

DAILY LECTIONARY

This outline is a devotional reading plan that covers the entire Sacred Scriptures each year. The selections are based on ancient models and are generally in harmony with the liturgical church year. The average reading is three chapters daily. A seasonal canticle is assigned for each month and is scheduled to replace the psalm on the first and last days of the month. All of the psalms are read twice a year.

The lectionary is in accordance with Martin Luther's suggestions: "But let the entire Psalter, divided in parts, remain in use and the entire Scriptures, divided into lections, let this be preserved in the ears of the church." Also: "After that another book should be selected, and so on, until the entire Bible has been read through, and where one does not understand it, pass that by and glorify God."

December

1 Luke 1:46–55
Revelation 1–2
2 Psalm 1
Revelation 3–5
3 Psalm 2
Revelation 6–8
4 Psalm 3
Revelation 9–11
5 Psalm 4
Revelation 12–14
6 Psalm 5
Revelation 15–17
7 Psalm 6
Revelation 18–20
8 Psalm 7
Revelation 21–22
9 Psalm 8
Isaiah 1–3
10 Psalm 9
Isaiah 4–6
11 Psalm 10
Isaiah 7–9
12 Psalm 11
Isaiah 10–12
13 Psalm 12
Isaiah 13–15
14 Psalm 13
Isaiah 16–18
15 Psalm 14
Isaiah 19–21
16 Psalm 15
Isaiah 22–24
17 Psalm 16
Isaiah 25–27
18 Psalm 17
Isaiah 28–30
19 Psalm 18
Isaiah 31–33
20 Psalm 19
Isaiah 34–36
21 Psalm 20
Isaiah 37–39
22 Psalm 21
Isaiah 40–42
23 Psalm 22
Isaiah 43–45
24 Psalm 23
Isaiah 46–48
25 Psalm 24
Isaiah 49–51
26 Psalm 25
Isaiah 52–54
27 Psalm 26
Isaiah 55–57
28 Psalm 27
Isaiah 58–60
29 Psalm 28
Isaiah 61–63
30 Psalm 29
Isaiah 64–66
31 Luke 1:46–55
Mark 1

January

1 Luke 1:68–79
Mark 2
2 Psalm 30
Mark 3
3 Psalm 31
Mark 4
4 Psalm 32
Mark 5
5 Psalm 33
Mark 6
6 Psalm 34
Mark 7
7 Psalm 35
Mark 8
8 Psalm 36
Mark 9
9 Psalm 37
Mark 10
10 Psalm 38
Mark 11
11 Psalm 39
Mark 12
12 Psalm 40
Mark 13
13 Psalm 41
Mark 14
14 Psalm 42
Mark 15–16
15 Psalm 43
Genesis 1–3
16 Psalm 44
Genesis 4–6
17 Psalm 45
Genesis 7–9
18 Psalm 46
Genesis 10–12
19 Psalm 47
Genesis 13–15
20 Psalm 48
Genesis 16–18
21 Psalm 49
Genesis 19–21
22 Psalm 50
Genesis 22–24
23 Psalm 51
Genesis 25–27
24 Psalm 52
Genesis 28–30
25 Psalm 53
Genesis 31–33
26 Psalm 54
Genesis 34–36
27 Psalm 55
Genesis 37–39
28 Psalm 56
Genesis 40–42
29 Psalm 57
Genesis 43–45
30 Psalm 58
Genesis 46–48
31 Luke 1:68–79
Genesis 49–50

February

1 Luke 2:29–32
Exodus 1–3
2 Psalm 59
Exodus 4–6
3 Psalm 60
Exodus 7–9
4 Psalm 61
Exodus 10–12
5 Psalm 62
Exodus 13–15
6 Psalm 63
Exodus 16–18
7 Psalm 64
Exodus 19–21

8 Psalm 65
Exodus 22–24
9 Psalm 66
Exodus 25–27
10 Psalm 67
Exodus 28–30
11 Psalm 68
Exodus 31–33
12 Psalm 69
Exodus 34–36
13 Psalm 70
Exodus 37–38
14 Psalm 71
Exodus 39–40
15 Psalm 72
Leviticus 1–3
16 Psalm 73
Leviticus 4–6
17 Psalm 74
Leviticus 7–9
18 Psalm 75
Leviticus 10–12
19 Psalm 76
Leviticus 13–15
20 Psalm 77
Leviticus 16–18
21 Psalm 78
Leviticus 19–21
22 Psalm 79
Leviticus 22–24
23 Psalm 80
Leviticus 25–27
24 Psalm 81
Numbers 1–3
25 Psalm 82
Numbers 4–6
26 Psalm 83
Numbers 7–9
27 Psalm 84
Numbers 10–12
28 Luke 2:29–32
Numbers 13–15

March

1 Isaiah 64:1–9
Numbers 16–18
2 Psalm 85
Numbers 19–21
3 Psalm 86
Numbers 22–24
4 Psalm 87
Numbers 25–27
5 Psalm 88
Numbers 28–30
6 Psalm 89
Numbers 31–33
7 Psalm 90
Numbers 34–36
8 Psalm 91
Deuteronomy 1–3
9 Psalm 92
Deuteronomy 4–6
10 Psalm 93
Deuteronomy 7–9
11 Psalm 94
Deuteronomy 10–12
12 Psalm 95
Deuteronomy 13–15
13 Psalm 96
Deuteronomy 16–18
14 Psalm 97
Deuteronomy 19–21
15 Psalm 98
Deuteronomy 22–24
16 Psalm 99
Deuteronomy 25–27
17 Psalm 100
Deuteronomy 28–30
18 Psalm 101
Deuteronomy 31–34
19 Psalm 102
Luke 1
20 Psalm 103
Luke 2–3
21 Psalm 104
Luke 4–5
22 Psalm 105
Luke 6–7
23 Psalm 106
Luke 8–9
24 Psalm 107
Luke 10–11
25 Psalm 108
Luke 12–13
26 Psalm 109
Luke 14–15
27 Psalm 110
Luke 16–17
28 Psalm 111
Luke 18–19
29 Psalm 112
Luke 20–21
30 Psalm 113
Luke 22
31 Isaiah 64:1–9
Luke 23–24

April

1 Isaiah 25:1–9
Romans 1–3
2 Psalm 114
Romans 4–6
3 Psalm 115
Romans 7–9
4 Psalm 116
Romans 10–13
5 Psalm 117
Romans 14–16
6 Psalm 118
1 Corinthians 1–3
7 Psalm 119:1–8
1 Corinthians 4–6
8 Psalm 119:9–16
1 Corinthians 7–9
9 Psalm 119:17–24
1 Corinthians 10–11
10 Psalm 119:25–32
1 Corinthians 12–14
11 Psalm 119:33–40
1 Corinthians 15–16
12 Psalm 119:41–48
2 Corinthians 1–4
13 Psalm 119:49–56
2 Corinthians 5–7
14 Psalm 119:57–64
2 Corinthians 8–10
15 Psalm 119:65–72
2 Corinthians 11–13
16 Psalm 119:73–80
Galatians 1–3
17 Psalm 119:81–88
Galatians 4–6
18 Psalm 119:89–96
Ephesians 1–3
19 Psalm 119:97–104
Ephesians 4–6
20 Psalm 119:105–112
Philippians 1–2
21 Psalm 119:113–120
Philippians 3–4
22 Psalm 119:121–128
Colossians 1–2
23 Psalm 119:129–136
Colossians 3–4
24 Psalm 119:137–144
1 Thessalonians 1–3
25 Psalm 119:145–152
1 Thessalonians 4–5
26 Psalm 119:153–160
2 Thessalonians 1–3
27 Psalm 119:161–168
1 Timothy 1–3
28 Psalm 119:169–176
1 Timothy 4–6
29 Psalm 120
2 Timothy 1–2
30 Isaiah 25:1–9
2 Timothy 3–4

May

1 Samuel 2:1–10
Titus, Philemon
2 Psalm 121
Hebrews 1–4
3 Psalm 122
Hebrews 5–7
4 Psalm 123
Hebrews 8–10
5 Psalm 124
Hebrews 11–13
6 Psalm 125
James 1–3
7 Psalm 126
James 4–5
8 Psalm 127
1 Peter 1–2
9 Psalm 128
1 Peter 3–5
10 Psalm 129
2 Peter
11 Psalm 130
1 John 1–3
12 Psalm 131
1 John 4–5
13 Psalm 132
2 John, 3 John, Jude
14 Psalm 133
John 1–2
15 Psalm 134
John 3–4

16 Psalm 135
John 5–6
17 Psalm 136
John 7–8
18 Psalm 137
John 9–10
19 Psalm 138
John 11–12
20 Psalm 139
John 13–14
21 Psalm 140
John 15–16
22 Psalm 141
John 17–18
23 Psalm 142
John 19
24 Psalm 143
John 20–21
25 Psalm 144
Acts 1–2
26 Psalm 145
Acts 3–4
27 Psalm 146
Acts 5–6
28 Psalm 147
Acts 7–8
29 Psalm 148
Acts 9–10
30 Psalm 149
Acts 11–12
31 1 Samuel 2:1–10
Acts 13–14

June

1 Isaiah 12:1–6
Acts 15–16
2 Psalm 150
Acts 17–18
3 Psalm 1
Acts 19–20
4 Psalm 2
Acts 21–22
5 Psalm 3
Acts 23–24
6 Psalm 4
Acts 25–26
7 Psalm 5
Acts 27–28
8 Psalm 6
Joshua 1–5
9 Psalm 7
Joshua 6–8
10 Psalm 8
Joshua 9–11
11 Psalm 9
Joshua 12–16
12 Psalm 10
Joshua 17–21
13 Psalm 11
Joshua 22–24
14 Psalm 12
Judges 1–3
15 Psalm 13
Judges 4–6
16 Psalm 14
Judges 7–9
17 Psalm 15
Judges 10–12
18 Psalm 16
Judges 13–15
19 Psalm 17
Judges 16–18
20 Psalm 18
Judges 19–21
21 Psalm 19
Ruth
22 Psalm 20
1 Samuel 1–3
23 Psalm 21
1 Samuel 4–6
24 Psalm 22
1 Samuel 7–9
25 Psalm 23
1 Samuel 10–12
26 Psalm 24
1 Samuel 13–15
27 Psalm 25
1 Samuel 16–18
28 Psalm 26
1 Samuel 19–21
29 Psalm 27
1 Samuel 22–24
30 Isaiah 12:1–6
1 Samuel 25–27

July

1 Deuteronomy 32:1–4
1 Samuel 28–31
2 Psalm 28
2 Samuel 1–3
3 Psalm 29
2 Samuel 4–6
4 Psalm 30
2 Samuel 7–9
5 Psalm 31
2 Samuel 10–12
6 Psalm 32
2 Samuel 13–15
7 Psalm 33
2 Samuel 16–18
8 Psalm 34
2 Samuel 19–21
9 Psalm 35
2 Samuel 22–24
10 Psalm 36
1 Kings 1–2
11 Psalm 37
1 Kings 3–6
12 Psalm 38
1 Kings 7–8
13 Psalm 39
1 Kings 9–11
14 Psalm 40
1 Kings 12–14
15 Psalm 41
1 Kings 15–17
16 Psalm 42
1 Kings 18–20
17 Psalm 43
1 Kings 21–22
18 Psalm 44
2 Kings 1–3
19 Psalm 45
2 Kings 4–6
20 Psalm 46
2 Kings 7–9
21 Psalm 47
2 Kings 10–12
22 Psalm 48
2 Kings 13–15
23 Psalm 49
2 Kings 16–18
24 Psalm 50
2 Kings 19–22
25 Psalm 51
2 Kings 23–25
26 Psalm 52
1 Chronicles 1–5
27 Psalm 53
1 Chronicles 6–10
28 Psalm 54
1 Chronicles 11–15
29 Psalm 55
1 Chronicles 16–20
30 Psalm 56
1 Chronicles 21–25
31 Deuteronomy 32:1–4
1 Chronicles 26–29

August

1 Habakkuk 3:2–19
2 Chronicles 1–3
2 Psalm 57
2 Chronicles 4–6
3 Psalm 58
2 Chronicles 7–9
4 Psalm 59
2 Chronicles 10–12
5 Psalm 60
2 Chronicles 13–15
6 Psalm 61
2 Chronicles 16–18
7 Psalm 62
2 Chronicles 19–21
8 Psalm 63
2 Chronicles 22–24
9 Psalm 64
2 Chronicles 25–27
10 Psalm 65
2 Chronicles 28–30
11 Psalm 66
2 Chronicles 31–33
12 Psalm 67
2 Chronicles 34–36
13 Psalm 68
Ezra 1–5
14 Psalm 69
Ezra 6–10
15 Psalm 70
Nehemiah 1–3
16 Psalm 71
Nehemiah 4–6
17 Psalm 72
Nehemiah 7–9
18 Psalm 73
Nehemiah 10–13
19 Psalm 74
Esther 1–3
20 Psalm 75
Esther 4–6
21 Psalm 76
Esther 7–10
22 Psalm 77
Job 1–3
23 Psalm 78
Job 4–6
24 Psalm 79
Job 7–9

25 Psalm 80
Job 10–12
26 Psalm 81
Job 13–15
27 Psalm 82
Job 16–18
28 Psalm 83
Job 19–21
29 Psalm 84
Job 22–24
30 Psalm 85
Job 25–27
31 Habakkuk 3:2–19
Job 28–30

September

1 1 Chronicles 29:10–13
Job 31–33
2 Psalm 86
Job 34–36
3 Psalm 87
Job 37–39
4 Psalm 88
Job 40–42
5 Psalm 89
Proverbs 1–3
6 Psalm 90
Proverbs 4–7
7 Psalm 91
Proverbs 8–10
8 Psalm 92
Proverbs 11–13
9 Psalm 93
Proverbs 14–16
10 Psalm 94
Proverbs 17–19
11 Psalm 95
Proverbs 20–22
12 Psalm 96
Proverbs 23–25
13 Psalm 97
Proverbs 26–28
14 Psalm 98
Proverbs 29–31
15 Psalm 99
Ecclesiastes 1–3
16 Psalm 100
Ecclesiastes 4–6
17 Psalm 101
Ecclesiastes 7–9
18 Psalm 102
Ecclesiastes 10–12
19 Psalm 103
Song of Solomon 1–4
20 Psalm 104
Song of Solomon 5–8
21 Psalm 105
Jeremiah 1–3
22 Psalm 106
Jeremiah 4–6
23 Psalm 107
Jeremiah 7–9
24 Psalm 108
Jeremiah 10–12
25 Psalm 109
Jeremiah 13–15
26 Psalm 110
Jeremiah 16–18
27 Psalm 111
Jeremiah 19–22
28 Psalm 112
Jeremiah 23–25
29 Psalm 113
Jeremiah 26–28
30 1 Chronicles 29:10–13
Jeremiah 29–31

October

1 Jonah 2:2–9
Jeremiah 32–34
2 Psalm 114
Jeremiah 35–37
3 Psalm 115
Jeremiah 38–40
4 Psalm 116
Jeremiah 41–43
5 Psalm 117
Jeremiah 44–47
6 Psalm 118
Jeremiah 48–50
7 Psalm 119:1–8
Jeremiah 51–52
8 Psalm 119:9–16
Lamentations 1–2
9 Psalm 119:17–24
Lamentations 3–5
10 Psalm 119:25–32
Ezekiel 1–3
11 Psalm 119:33–40
Ezekiel 4–6
12 Psalm 119:41–48
Ezekiel 7–9
13 Psalm 119:49–56
Ezekiel 10–12
14 Psalm 119:57–64
Ezekiel 13–15
15 Psalm 119:65–72
Ezekiel 16–18
16 Psalm 119:73–80
Ezekiel 19–21
17 Psalm 119:81–88
Ezekiel 22–24
18 Psalm 119:89–96
Ezekiel 25–27
19 Psalm 119:97–104
Ezekiel 28–30
20 Psalm 119:105–112
Ezekiel 31–33
21 Psalm 119:113–120
Ezekiel 34–36
22 Psalm 119:121–128
Ezekiel 37–39
23 Psalm 119:129–136
Ezekiel 40–42
24 Psalm 119:137–144
Ezekiel 43–45
25 Psalm 119:145–152
Ezekiel 46–48
26 Psalm 119:153–160
Daniel 1–3
27 Psalm 119:161–168
Daniel 4–6
28 Psalm 119:169–176
Daniel 7–9
29 Psalm 120
Daniel 10–12
30 Psalm 121
Hosea 1–4
31 Jonah 2:2–9
Hosea 5–7

November

1 Exodus 15:1–18
Hosea 8–10
2 Psalm 122
Hosea 11–14
3 Psalm 123
Joel
4 Psalm 124
Amos 1–5
5 Psalm 125
Amos 6–9
6 Psalm 126
Obadiah, Jonah
7 Psalm 127
Micah 1–3
8 Psalm 128
Micah 4–7
9 Psalm 129
Nahum
10 Psalm 130
Habakkuk
11 Psalm 131
Zephaniah
12 Psalm 132
Haggai
13 Psalm 133
Zechariah 1–5
14 Psalm 134
Zechariah 6–10
15 Psalm 135
Zechariah 11–14
16 Psalm 136
Malachi
17 Psalm 137
Matthew 1–2
18 Psalm 138
Matthew 3–4
19 Psalm 139
Matthew 5–6
20 Psalm 140
Matthew 7–8
21 Psalm 141
Matthew 9–10
22 Psalm 142
Matthew 11–12
23 Psalm 143
Matthew 13–14
24 Psalm 144
Matthew 15–16
25 Psalm 145
Matthew 17–18
26 Psalm 146
Matthew 19–20
27 Psalm 147
Matthew 21–22
28 Psalm 148
Matthew 23–24
29 Psalm 149–150
Matthew 25–26
30 Exodus 15:1–18
Matthew 27–28

How We Got Our Bible

1. The Bible Jesus Knew

In Jesus' time every Jewish community had the part of our Bible we call the Old Testament. It was handwritten on scrolls, in Hebrew and Aramaic, and kept in the synagogue, where people met for religious instruction and worship. Jesus read from a scroll like this in the synagogue at Nazareth (Luke 4:16–20).

The scrolls were made from goatskins or sheepskins, sewed together to make rolls, each from 10 to 30 feet long. Usually each scroll contained a book. The Old Testament was written first in Hebrew and Aramaic, but by the time of Christ had been translated into the international language, Greek. This Greek translation of the Old Testament is called the Septuagint.

2. The Good News

The New Testament tells the Good News of Jesus Christ and describes experiences of the early Christians. While Greek is the language of the books of the New Testament, some of Jesus' words are recorded in transliterated Aramaic in the New Testament, indicating that Jesus often spoke in Aramaic.

Much of the New Testament consists of letters written by Paul and others to early Christian churches. Copies of these and of the gospel writings were widely circulated among neighboring churches.

3. A Translation into Latin—A.D. 410

Jerome, a scholar appointed by the bishop of Rome, worked 25 years to translate the entire Bible from Hebrew, Aramaic, and Greek into Latin, the language of the church and the well-educated in the Western world at that time. The Vulgate, Jerome's translation, is still the official text of the Roman Catholic Church.

The term *Vulgate* comes from the Latin word meaning "common" or "ordinary." First applied to Jerome's Bible in the 13th century, the title of the Vulgate refers to the frequent and common use made of it by the church and to the fact that Latin was the common language of the educated at Jerome's time.

4. Martin Luther—A.D. 1483–1546

Martin Luther asserted the Bible's supremacy. Defying church and state he declared his conscience was governed only by the Word of God. To bring the Bible to all the people, he prepared a German translation of the New Testament in 1522, and of the whole Bible in 1534.

Luther used vivid, everyday expressions to make the meaning clear and alive, and in making his translation he referred to the original Hebrew and Greek. His work had considerable influence on English translations that followed.

5. William Tyndale—A.D. 1494–1536

William Tyndale was the first and most influential of the great 16th-century English translators. Many of his expressions survive in the Bible we read today. Tyndale felt that the people had a right to know what God promised them in the Scriptures, but the Latin Bible was the only one then available to most Englishmen. Most common people could not read Latin. Few were able to obtain one of the scarce, handwritten copies of the old English translation by John Wycliffe (1330–1384). Even fewer could read its text, for the language had changed much in 150 years. Tyndale knew that only a new translation, written in the English of his day, could satisfy the people's hunger for the Scriptures.

6. The First Printed English New Testament—A.D. 1525

Johannes Gutenberg, the inventor of printing, produced the first printed Bible (in Latin) about 1456. Tyndale's New Testament was the first to be printed in English. It was done in Germany, because the translation and its use were prohibited in England by both the king and the church. Copies were smuggled into England in shipments of grain and cloth. Tyndale was working on a translation of the Old Testament when he was betrayed and condemned to be strangled and burned. His last words were a prayer: "Lord, open Thou the King of England's eyes."

7. The King James Version—A.D. 1611

At a conference called by King James in 1604 to consider, among other things, the serious differences of opinion over versions of the Bible, Dr. John Reynolds proposed a new translation that would have the approval of the whole church. A group of 54 scholars were appointed to undertake such a revision. They based their work on a study of early Hebrew and Greek manuscripts as well as on many of the later translations, and much thought was given to beauty of style. The new Bible immediately replaced the versions then being used in the churches. Within the next 50 years it became the most popular version for use in the home.

8. The New International Version—A.D. 1973–1984

The New International Version (NIV) is one of a number of recent translations that are accurate and faithful to original texts. The New International Version is a completely new translation of the Holy Bible made by more than 100 scholars working directly from the best available Hebrew, Aramaic, and Greek texts. The fact that participants from the United States, Great Britain, Canada, Australia, and New Zealand worked together gave the project its international scope.

As time goes on, more revisions will be made, perfecting and clarifying the translations but not changing the great history of the great truth the Bible brings to us—our most precious heritage.

Heaven and earth will pass away, but My words will never pass away. Matthew 24:35

A Prayer Before Reading the Scripture

Blessed Lord, since You have caused all Holy Scriptures to be written for our learning, grant that we may so hear them, read, mark, learn, and take them to heart that by patience and comfort of Your Holy Word we may embrace and ever hold fast the blessed hope of everlasting life; through Jesus Christ, Your Son, our Lord, who lives and reigns with You and the Holy Spirit, one God, now and forever. Amen.

a prayer of the ancient church